Library of Congress Cataloging-in-Publication Data

Backman, Milton Vaughn.
    Joseph Smith and the Doctrine & Covenants / Milton V. Backman, Jr., Richard O. Cowan.
      p. cm.
    Includes bibliographical references and index.
    ISBN 0-87579-653-2
    1. Doctrine and covenants—Commentaries. 2. Smith, Joseph, 1805–1844. 3. Private revelations. I. Cowan, Richard O., 1934–.
II. Title.
BX8628.B38   1992
289.3′2–dc20   92-33120
                                                    CIP

Printed in the United States of America

10   9   8   7   6   5   4   3   2   1

CONTENTS

LIST OF MAPS

PREFACE

The Doctrine and Covenants is unique even among our standard works. The other scriptural books blend a historical narrative with their great doctrinal principles. Their teachings take on added meaning as they are seen in the context of the needs and experiences of God's people at the time. The Doctrine and Covenants, however, is almost entirely a collection of revelations. Hence, we must turn to other sources for insights from the historical background.

In conjunction with the Religious Studies Center at Brigham Young University, Dr. Milton V. Backman, Jr., has compiled on computer more than one hundred fifty diaries, journals, and other firsthand accounts from early Latter-day Saints who lived during the time of the Prophet Joseph Smith. This database, entitled "Writings of Early Latter-day Saints and Their Contemporaries," is available in the Harold B. Lee Library at Brigham Young University. Spelling, punctuation, and grammar in these documents have been standardized to current usage to make these writings more understandable. Other eyewitness accounts are drawn from published sources and are reproduced here exactly as published, unless otherwise indicated. Dr. Richard O. Cowan has identified items from the database and other sources that particularly shed light on Doctrine and Covenants scriptures. Both authors have worked together to select quotations for this work and to provide introductory material necessary to explain their relevance to the Doctrine and Covenants.

The authors hope that the content of this volume will be a blessing to teachers and students of the Doctrine and Covenants. Statements written by eyewitnesses shed light on the background and historical context of the Lord's revelations. Seeing these events through the eyes of those who actually participated in them should help us better appreciate the revelations and how they can apply to our lives today.

The authors express appreciation to all who have helped bring this work to completion. Brigham Young University provided facilities, equipment, and other support that made this project possible. Many student secretaries and researchers provided valuable and necessary assistance. Junius Merrill worked closely with the authors in selecting and preparing the quotations to be included and also in refining the text of the twenty-six chapters in this book. Special gratitude is given to Barbara Crawley, Debbie Boone, and James Shumway, secretaries in the Religious Studies Center, who helped prepare the manuscript. Now that their work is completed, the authors hope it will be of special benefit to you, the reader.

1

HOW THE DOCTRINE AND COVENANTS CAME TO BE

Doctrine and Covenants 1

Revelation through living prophets provides a significant foundation for the faith of the Latter-day Saints. Modern-day divine communications began with the personal appearance of the Father and the Son to Joseph Smith in the early spring of 1820 and have continued to guide the Church ever since. The first step in recognizing these revelations as official scripture came just two months after the Church was organized. At a conference held in Fayette, New York, on 9 June 1830, Joseph Smith read the "Articles and Covenants" (now Doctrine and Covenants 20 and 22), which set forth the basic doctrines, organizations, and procedures of the newly restored Church, and they were accepted unanimously.

PREPARATIONS TO PUBLISH THE BOOK OF COMMANDMENTS

Initially, the Prophet did not record his revelations at the time he received them, but the Lord instructed him in July 1830 to "continue calling upon God in my name, and writing the things which shall be given thee" (D&C 24:5). Joseph immediately began "copying and arranging the revelations received up to that time, evidently with a view to their publication in book form" (D&C, 1921 ed., p. iii). Parley P. Pratt, who was present when several of these divine communications were given, described how the Prophet received them: "Each sentence was uttered slowly and very distinctly, and with a pause between each, sufficiently long for it to be recorded, by an ordinary writer, in long hand. This was the manner in which all his written revelations were dictated and written. There was never any hesitation, reviewing, or reading back, in order to keep the run of the subject" (*Autobiography*, p. 62). William E. McLellin, another close associate, likewise recalled: "I, as scribe, have written revelations from the mouth of [the Prophet]. And I have been present many times when others wrote for Joseph; therefore I speak as one having experience. The scribe seats himself at a desk or table, with pen, ink, and paper. The subject of enquiry being understood, the Prophet and Revelator enquires of God. He spiritually sees, hears, and feels, and then speaks as he is moved upon by the Holy Ghost, the 'thus saith the Lord,' sentence after sentence, and waits for his amanuenses to write and then read aloud each sentence. Thus they proceed until the revelator says Amen, at the close of what is then communicated. I have known [Joseph], without premeditation, to thus deliver off in broken sentences, some of the most sublime pieces of composition which I ever perused in any book" (*Ensign of Liberty*, pp. 98–99).

Of the revelations recorded in the Doctrine and Covenants, some thirty-seven sections, more than one-fourth of the total, were received during 1831 alone. These revelations were copied by hand for the use of the early Saints, but demand for them grew. Therefore, at a conference in November 1831, the Church considered publishing the "Book of Commandments." During that conference the Lord revealed what is now Doctrine and Covenants 1 to be "my preface unto the book of my commandments" (D&C 1:6). An early Latter-day Saint cited Oliver Cowdery's account of what happened on that occasion: "A committee had been appointed to draft a preface, consisting of . . . O. Cowdery and, I think, Sidney Rigdon, but when they made their report . . . the Conference then requested Joseph to enquire of the Lord about it, and he said that he would if the people would bow in prayer with him. This they did and Joseph prayed.

"When they arose, Joseph dictated by the Spirit the preface found in the Book of Doctrine and Covenants while sitting by a window of the room [John Johnson home in Hiram, Ohio] in which the conference was sitting; and Sidney Rigdon wrote it down. Joseph would deliver a few sentences and Sidney would write them down, then read them aloud, and if correct, then Joseph would proceed and deliver more, and by this process the preface was given" (William Kelley, in *Saints Herald*, 16 Jan. 1882, p. 67). At this point, William E. McLellin voiced some concerns about the wording of the Prophet's revelations. In response, the Lord issued the challenge quoted in Doctrine and Covenants 67:5–8. "After the foregoing was received," Joseph wrote in his history, "William E. M'Lellin, as the wisest man, in his own estimation, having more learning than sense, endeavored to write a commandment like unto one of the least of the Lord's, but failed; it was an awful responsibility to write in the name of the Lord. The Elders and all present that witnessed this vain attempt of a man to imitate the language of Jesus Christ, renewed their faith in the fulness of the Gospel, and in the truth of the commandments and revelations which the Lord had given to the Church through my instrumentality" (*History of the Church*, 1:226). Consequently, the conference decided to print several thousand copies of the revelations. Before the conference adjourned, the Lord also revealed what is now Doctrine and Covenants 133 to be an "appendix" for the book.

The revelations were to be printed on a press that would also publish a Latter-day Saint newspaper in Independence, Missouri. By the summer of 1833 the project of publishing the revelations was nearing completion. Then, on July 20, a mob broke into William W. Phelps's home and destroyed the press. Through the quick and courageous action of Church members who happened to be at the scene, several hundred of the unbound sheets were rescued. Mary Rollins Lightner, who was a teenager at the time, recalled the attack: "The mob renewed their efforts again by tearing down the printing office, a two story building, and driving Brother Phelps' family out of the lower part of the house and putting their things in the street. They brought out some large sheets of paper, and said, 'Here are the Mormon Commandments.' My sister Caroline and myself were in a corner of a fence watching them; when they spoke of the commandments I was determined to have some of them. Sister said if I went to get any of them she would go too, but said 'they will kill us.' While their backs were turned, prying out the gable end of the house, we went, and got our arms full, and were turning away, when some of the mob saw us and called on us to stop, but we ran as fast as we could. Two of them started after us. Seeing a gap in a fence, we entered into a large cornfield, laid the papers on the ground, and hid them with our persons. The corn was from five to six feet high, and very thick; they hunted around considerable, and came very near us but did not find us" ("Autobiography," *Utah Genealogical and Historical Magazine*, July 1926, p. 196). The Saints cherished and bound the few copies they were able to save. The revelations in the Book of Commandments roughly paralleled the first sixty-four sections of our present Doctrine and Covenants, but we do not know how many other revelations might have been included if the printing had not been disrupted.

THE DOCTRINE AND COVENANTS

Not long after the destruction of the press in 1833, steps were taken to publish an even larger compilation, the Prophet having received additional significant revelations. On 17 August 1835, a solemn assembly convened to accept this expanded volume. The new title, "Doctrine and Covenants," reflected the two rather distinct parts of the book: the seven Lectures on Faith, prepared for use in the School of the Prophets during the 1834–35 season, treated the "doctrine of the Church"; and revelations, commonly referred to as the "Covenants and Commandments," completed the volume. The 1835 edition added forty-five new revelations. Another important change was made in the "Covenants" section: revelations had been called chapters in the Book of Commandments; now they were known as sections.

Forty-one years later, a significant new edition of the Doctrine and Covenants added to the scriptural canon a total of twenty-five revelations given through Joseph Smith between thirty-three and fifty-three years earlier. Under Brigham Young's direction, Orson Pratt arranged the revelations in essentially a chronological order, and introduced the present verse divisions. These features made the new book much easier to study and reference.

An important addition to the Doctrine and Covenants was made just after the turn of the century. President Wilford Woodruff's 1890 "Official Declaration," or "Manifesto," ending the performance of plural marriages was incorporated into the Doctrine and Covenants beginning with the 1908 printing. In England, a page bearing the Manifesto was glued into copies of the book that had been printed there two years earlier (Woodford, "Historical Development of the Doctrine and Covenants," pp. 92–93).

The 1921 edition of the Doctrine and Covenants introduced easier-to-read, double-columned pages, and improved section headings. The most significant change was the deletion of the Lectures on Faith, which had been published with the revelations since 1835. The introduction to the 1921 edition explained that this material was "never presented to nor accepted by the Church as being otherwise than theological lectures or lessons."

OUR PRESENT EDITION

In 1981, for the first time in more than a century, numbered sections were added to the Doctrine and Covenants. Section 137, the revelation in which Joseph Smith learned that those who died without hearing the gospel might still have an opportunity to inherit the celestial kingdom, and section 138, Joseph F. Smith's vision of how the Savior inaugurated the preaching of the gospel in the spirit world, both set forth the fundamentals of salvation for the dead. These two revelations were added to the Doctrine and Covenants at a time of unprecedented temple building and activity, illustrating how the scriptural canon may be enlarged to meet a particular need at a particular time.

Another addition was Official Declaration 2, announcing President Spencer W. Kimball's 1978 revelation extending the blessings of the priesthood to all races. This revelation was received at a time of worldwide Church growth. As was the case with Official Declaration 1, or Wilford Woodruff's Manifesto, Official Declaration 2 is not a record of the revelation itself but rather an inspired announcement that the revelation had been received. That may explain why these two documents have the unique status of Official Declarations rather than being included with the numbered sections of the Doctrine and Covenants.

Expanded historical notes and more specific content summaries enhanced the section headings in the new edition. An easier-to-follow cross-referencing system improved the usefulness of the new volume of scripture in gospel study. President Spencer W. Kimball gave those preparing this new edition the charge " 'to assist in improving doctrinal scholarship throughout the Church.' The goal of everyone involved has been to put into the hands of the members of the Church the tools that will enable them better to study and understand the Lord's revelations through his prophets" *(Ensign,* Oct. 1981, p. 9).

2

JOSEPH SMITH RECEIVES THE PLATES AND BEGINS TRANSLATING

Doctrine and Covenants 2; 3; 10

The three sections in the Doctrine and Covenants received the earliest all relate to Joseph Smith's learning about the Book of Mormon and beginning to translate that sacred record.

VISITS BY THE ANGEL MORONI

On the night of 21–22 September 1823, an angel named Moroni appeared to Joseph Smith three times. During these visitations Joseph learned that by the power of God he would translate the Book of Mormon (Joseph Smith–History 1:34). Nearly two decades later, in his famous letter to newspaper editor John Wentworth, the Prophet wrote that Moroni had proclaimed "that the preparatory work for the second coming of the Messiah was speedily to commence; that the time was at hand for the Gospel in all its fullness to be preached in power, unto all nations that a people might be prepared for the Millennial reign" (*History of the Church*, 4:537). Moroni quoted several passages of scripture relating to these last days to emphasize the importance of preparing for them. Doctrine and Covenants 2 contains his paraphrase of Malachi 4:5–6 about the coming of Elijah. (See Joseph Smith–History 1:30–53 for additional information on Moroni's three appearances that night and two more that occurred the next day.)

Oliver Cowdery, a close associate of the Prophet, described in an early account of these visions the temptation, chastisement, and repentance Joseph experienced when he met Moroni at Cumorah. As he walked to the hill, "two invisible powers were operating upon his mind." One urged him to obey explicitly the instructions of the angel and the other to use the record for personal gain. When Joseph arrived at the hill, "on attempting to take possession of the record a shock was produced upon his system, by an invisible power which deprived him, in a measure, of his natural strength. . . . he exclaimed, 'Why can I not obtain this book?' 'Because you have not kept the commandments of the Lord,' answered a voice, within a seeming short distance. He looked, and to his astonishment, there stood the angel who had previously given him the directions concerning this matter.

"At that instant he looked to the Lord in prayer, and as he prayed darkness began to disperse from his mind and his soul was lit up as it was the evening before, and he was filled with the Holy Spirit. . . . While he thus stood gazing and admiring, the angel said, 'Look!' and as he thus spake he beheld the prince of darkness, surrounded by his innumerable train of associates. All this passed before him, and the heavenly messenger said, 'All this is shown, the good and the evil, the holy and impure, the glory of God and the power of darkness, that you may know hereafter the two powers and never be influenced or overcome by that wicked one. . . . You now see why you could not obtain this record; that the commandment was strict, and that if ever these sacred things are obtained they must be by prayer and faithfulness in obeying the Lord. They are not deposited here for the sake of accumulating gain and wealth for the glory of this world: they were sealed by the prayer of faith, and because of the knowledge which they contain they are of no worth among the children of men, only for their knowledge. On them is contained the fulness of the gospel of Jesus Christ" (*Messenger and Advocate*, Oct. 1835, pp. 197–98).

During the evening following these visions, Joseph Smith told his family about his remarkable experiences. They believed what he related to them and were fascinated by his suddenly increased knowledge of life in ancient America. As his mother explained, "From this time forth, Joseph continued to receive instructions from the Lord, and we continued to get the children together every evening for the purpose of listening while he gave us a relation of the same. I presume our family presented an aspect as singular as any that ever lived upon the face of the earth — all seated in a circle, father, mother, sons and daughters, and giving the most profound attention to a boy, eighteen years of age, who had never read the Bible through in his life: he seemed much less inclined to the perusal of books than any of the rest of our children, but far more given to meditation and deep study.

"We were now confirmed in the opinion that God was about to

bring to light something upon which we could stay our minds, or that would give us a more perfect knowledge of the plan of salvation and the redemption of the human family. This caused us greatly to rejoice, the sweetest union and happiness pervaded our house, and tranquility reigned in our midst.

"During our evening conversations, Joseph would occasionally give us some of the most amusing recitals that could be imagined. He would describe the ancient inhabitants of this continent, their dress, mode of traveling, and the animals upon which they rode; their cities, their buildings, with every particular; their mode of warfare; and also their religious worship. This he would do with as much ease, seemingly, as if he had spent his whole life among them" (Lucy Smith, *History*, pp. 82–83).

The Prophet's brother William also described the family's emotions as they accepted Joseph's incredible accounts:

"The whole family were melted to tears, and believed all he said. Knowing that he was very young, that he had not enjoyed the advantages of a common education; and knowing too, his whole character and disposition, they were convinced that he was totally incapable of arising before his aged parents, his brothers and sisters, and so solemnly giving utterance to anything but the truth" (William Smith, *On Mormonism*, pp. 9–10).

THE LOST MANUSCRIPT

Moroni continued to tutor the young prophet for four years. After Joseph Smith obtained the gold plates from the angel in September 1827, persecution intensified. Consequently, in December, Joseph and Emma moved to Harmony, Pennsylvania, and located near her parents' home. There Joseph began translating the Book of Mormon with Emma serving as scribe. In February 1828, Martin Harris, a Palmyra farmer who had previously befriended and assisted the Prophet, traveled to Harmony to personally help with the work. In that same month, Martin also journeyed to New York City, where an ancient prophecy was fulfilled (see Joseph Smith–History 1:64–65).

A relatively unknown history written by Joseph Smith in 1832 points out that because of Martin's faith and his assisting Joseph in the move to Harmony, "the Lord appeared unto him in a vision and shewed unto him his marvilous work which he was about to do and ⟨he⟩ imediately came to Su[s]quehanna and said the Lord had shown

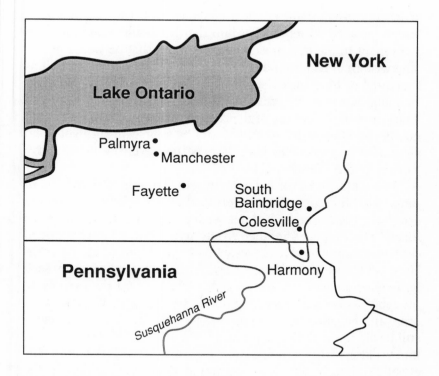

him that he must go to new York City with some of the c⟨h⟩aracters so we proceeded to coppy some of them and he took his Journy to the Eastern Cittys and to the Learned ⟨saying⟩ read this I pray thee and the learned said I cannot but if he wo = uld bring the plates they would read it but the Lord had fo⟨r⟩bid it and he returned to me and gave them to ⟨me to⟩ translate and I said . . . [I] cannot for I am not learned, but the Lord had prepared . . . spectacles for to read the Book therefore I commenced translating the char = acters and thus the Prop[h]icy of Is⟨ai⟩ah was fulfilled which is written in the 29 chapter concerning the book" (Jessee, *Personal Writings*, pp. 7–8).

In April 1828, Martin arranged his business affairs in Palmyra, returned to Harmony, and became a scribe for Joseph Smith. By June 14, the Prophet had dictated 116 pages of manuscript. Martin, on three separate occasions, asked Joseph for permission to take the manuscript to show to relatives and friends in Palmyra. The first two times, the Lord denied the request, but the third time granted it, if Martin would show the writings only to five specified members of his immediate family. "In accordance with this last answer," Joseph recorded, "I required of him that he should bind himself in a covenant to me in a most solemn manner that he would not do otherwise than had been directed. He did so. He bound himself as I required of him, took the writings, and went his way. Notwithstanding, however, the great restrictions which he had been laid under, and the solemnity of the covenant which he had made with me, he did show them to others, and by stratagem they got them away from him, and they never have been recovered unto this day" (*History of the Church*, 1:21).

When Martin Harris did not return to Harmony with the manuscript, Joseph became deeply concerned and traveled to Palmyra to determine the reason he had not received any information from his friend. The Prophet's mother vividly remembered Joseph's arrival early one morning: "He requested us to send immediately for Mr. Harris. This we did without delay. . . . he generally came in such haste when he was sent for. At eight o'clock we set the victuals on the table, as we were expecting him every moment. We waited till nine, and he came not—till ten, and he was not there—till eleven, still he did not make his appearance. But at half past twelve we saw him walking with a slow and measured tread towards the house, his eyes fixed thoughtfully upon the ground. On coming to the gate, he stopped, instead of passing through, and got upon the fence, and sat there some time with his hat drawn over his eyes. At length he entered the house. Soon after which we sat down to the table, Mr. Harris with the rest. He took up his knife and fork as if he were going to use them, but immediately dropped them. Hyrum, observing this, said 'Martin, why do you not eat; are you sick?' Upon which Mr. Harris pressed his hands upon his temples, and cried out in a tone of deep anguish, 'Oh, I have lost my soul! I have lost my soul!'

"Joseph who had not expressed his fears till now, sprang from the table, exclaiming, 'Martin, have you lost that manuscript? Have you broken your oath, and brought down condemnation upon my head as well as your own?'

" 'Yes; it is gone,' replied Martin, 'and I know not where.'

" 'Oh, my God!' said Joseph, clinching his hands. 'All is lost! all is lost! What shall I do? I have sinned—it is I who tempted the wrath of God. I should have been satisfied with the first answer which I received from the Lord; for he told me that it was not safe to let the writing go out of my possession.' He wept and groaned, and walked the floor continually.

"At length he told Martin to go back and search again.

" 'No'; said Martin, 'it is all in vain; for I have ripped open beds and pillows; and I know it is not there.'

" 'Then must I,' said Joseph, 'return with such a tale as this? I dare not do it. And how shall I appear before the Lord? Of what rebuke am I not worthy from the angel of the Most High?'

"I besought him not to mourn so, for perhaps the Lord would forgive him, after a short season of humiliation and repentance. But what could I do to comfort him, when he saw all the family in the same situation of mind as himself; for sobs and groans, and the most bitter lamentations filled the house. However, Joseph was more distressed than the rest, as he better understood the consequences of disobedience. And he continued pacing back and forth, meantime weeping and grieving, until about sunset, when, by persuasion, he took a little nourishment.

"The next morning, he set out for home [in Pennsylvania]. We parted with heavy hearts, for it now appeared that all which we had so fondly anticipated, and which had been the source of so much secret gratification, had in a moment fled, and fled forever" (Lucy Smith, *History,* pp. 127–29).

Joseph later told his mother what happened after his return to Harmony: "Soon after my arrival, I commenced humbling myself in mighty prayer before the Lord, and, as I was pouring out my soul in supplication to God, that if possible I might obtain mercy at his hands and be forgiven of all that I had done contrary to his will, an angel stood before me, and answered me, saying, that I had sinned in delivering the manuscript into the hands of a wicked man, and, as I had ventured to become responsible for his faithfulness, I would of necessity have to suffer the consequences of his indiscretion, and I must now give up the Urim and Thummim into his (the angel's) hands" (Lucy Smith, *History,* pp. 133–34).

A short time later, Joseph's history records, "I was walking out a little distance, when, behold, the former heavenly messenger appeared and handed to me the Urim and Thummim again—for it had been taken from me in consequence of my having wearied the Lord in asking for the privilege of letting Martin Harris take the writings, which he lost by transgression—and I inquired of the Lord through it, and obtained the following [see D&C 3].

"After I had obtained the above revelation, both the plates and the Urim and Thummim were taken from me again; but in a few days they were returned to me, when I inquired of the Lord" *(History of the Church,* 1:20–23). At that time he received the revelation (D&C 10) instructing him to continue translating.

3

THOSE WHO CAME TO JOSEPH'S AID

Doctrine and Covenants 4–9; 11–12; 14–16

Eleven revelations, recorded now in Doctrine and Covenants 4–9, 11–12, and 14–16, were given during the first half of 1829. They were addressed to various individuals who provided substantial assistance as Joseph completed the translation of the Book of Mormon. All recipients were directed to "thrust in their sickle" and labor to bring forth God's work. This instruction, first given to the Prophet's father (D&C 4), was repeated in several of these communications.

THE COMING OF OLIVER COWDERY

Even though he received the plates once again from the angel in the summer of 1828, Joseph did not resume the translation immediately but rather worked on his farm to support his family. Recalling some of the difficulties he encountered when he resumed translating, Joseph wrote, "Now my wife had writen some for me to translate and also my Brother Samuel H Smith but we had become reduced in property and my wives [wife's] father was about to turn me out of doors & I had not where to go and I cried unto the Lord that he would provide for me to accomplish the work whereunto he had commanded me" (Jessee, *Personal Writings*, p. 8).

The answer to Joseph's prayer was Oliver Cowdery, a school teacher temporarily boarding with the Smith family in Manchester, New York. He traveled approximately one hundred miles to Joseph Smith's home in Harmony, Pennsylvania. Joseph's 1832 history explained why Oliver was willing to make such a trip:

"[The] Lord appeared unto a young man by the name of Oliver Cowdry [Cowdery] and shewed unto him the plates in a vision and also the truth of the work and what the Lord was about to do through me his unworthy servant therefore he was desirous to come and write for me and translate" (Jessee, *Personal Writings*, p. 8).

Oliver arrived in Harmony on 5 April 1829, and two days later he became a scribe for Joseph Smith. During that month, four revelations were directed to Joseph and Oliver (D&C 6–9). In the first of these, the Lord referred to a spiritual experience that Oliver had had while still in Manchester (D&C 6:23–24). Joseph recalled that after receiving this revelation, Oliver confided to him the details of what had happened: "Oliver Cowdery stated to me that after he had gone to my father's to board, and after the family had communicated to him concerning my having obtained the plates, that one night after he had retired to bed he called upon the Lord to know if these things were so, and the Lord manifested to him that they were true, but he had kept the circumstance entirely secret, and had mentioned it to no one; so that after this revelation was given, he knew that the work was true, because no being living knew of the thing alluded to in the revelation, but God and himself" (*History of the Church,* 1:35).

The original manuscript of the Book of Mormon and the writings of Joseph Smith and Oliver Cowdery provide historical evidence that nearly all of the Book of Mormon was translated in less than three months. Between April and sometime in June 1829, Joseph dictated possibly an average of about eight pages a day.

Five years later, Oliver Cowdery described his feelings about his role in the coming forth of the Book of Mormon. "These were days never to be forgotten — to sit under the sound of a voice dictated by the inspiration of heaven, awakened the utmost gratitude of this bosom! Day after day I continued, uninterrupted, to write from his mouth, as he translated, with the Urim and Thummim, or, as the Nephites would have said, 'Interpreters,' the history, or record, called 'The Book of Mormon' " (*Messenger and Advocate,* Oct. 1834, p. 14).

Ten years after his excommunication, Oliver Cowdery rejoined the Saints, who were then in their exodus to the Great Basin. He bore a powerful testimony at a conference at Council Bluffs, Iowa, in 1848, regarding the divine origins of the Book of Mormon:

" 'Friends and brethren, — My name is Cowdery — Oliver Cowdery. In the early history of this Church I stood identified with her, and [was] one in her councils. True it is that the gifts and callings of God are without repentance. Not because I was better than the rest of mankind was I called; but, to fulfil the purposes of God, he called me to a high and holy calling. I wrote, with my own pen, the entire Book of Mormon (save a few pages,) as it fell from the lips of the Prophet Joseph Smith, as he translated it by the gift and power of God, by the means of the Urim and Thummim, or, as it is called by that book, 'holy interpreters.' I beheld with my eyes and handled with my hands the gold plates from which it was transcribed. I also saw with my eyes and handled with my hands the 'holy interpreters.' That book is *true*. Sidney Rigdon did not write it. Mr. Spaulding did not write it. I wrote it myself as it fell from the lips of the Prophet. It contains the everlasting Gospel, and came forth to the children of men in fulfilment of the revelations of John, where he says he saw an angel come with the everlasting Gospel to preach to every nation, kindred, tongue, and people. It contains principles of salvation; and if you, my hearers, will walk by its light and obey its precepts, you will be saved with an everlasting salvation in the kingdom of God" (*Millennial Star*, 20 Aug. 1859, p. 544).

OTHERS ASSIST WITH THE WORK

Two revelations (D&C 11–12), given at Harmony during May, were directed to Hyrum Smith and Joseph Knight, Sr., respectively. In various ways, the latter assisted the Prophet, who had started working for him in 1826. "I paid him the money," Knight wrote, "and I furnished him with a horse and Cutter to go and see his girl Down to Mr. Hails" (*BYU Studies*, Autumn 1976, p. 32). Joseph married Emma Hale on 18 January 1827.

According to Knight, the angel had told Joseph Smith that "if he would Do right according to the will of God he mite obtain [the plates] the 22nt Day of Septemper Next and if not he never would have them." Joseph Knight traveled to Manchester to be there on the appointed day. The following morning, Joseph Knight discovered his horse and buggy were missing, but soon the Prophet returned with them. "After Brackfirst [breakfast]," Knight recorded, "Joseph Cald me into the other Room and he set his foot on the Bed and leaned his head on his hand and says '. . . it is ten times Better then I expected.' Then he went on to tell the length and width and thickness of the plates, and said he, 'they appear to be Gold.' But he seamed to think more of the glasses or the urim and thummem then [than] he Did of the plates, for, says he, 'I can see any thing; they are Marvelus. Now they are writen in Caracters and I want them translated.'

"Now he was Commanded not to let no [any] one see those things But a few for witness at a givin time. Now it soon got about that Joseph Smith had found the plates and peopel Come in to see them But he told them that they Could not for he must not shoe [show] them. But many insisted and oferd money and Property to see them. But, for keeping them from the Peopel they persecuted and abused them [him] and they [the Smiths] ware obliged to hide them [the plates], and they hid them under a Brick harth in the west Room. . . .

"Now when he Began to translate [after moving to Harmony] he was poor and was put to it for provisions and had no one to write for him But his wife, and his wifes Brother [probably Reuben Hale] would sometimes write a little for him through the winter. . . .

" . . . His wifes father and familey ware all against him and would not h[e]lp him. He and his wife Came up to see me the first of the winter 1828 and told me his Case. But I was not in easy circumstances and I did not know what it mite amount to and my wife [Polly Knight] and familey all against me about helping him. But I let him have some little provisions and some few things out of the Store apair of shoes and three Dollars in money to help him a litle. . . . [The next spring] I told my wife I must go Dow[n] and see Joseph again. 'Why Do you go so soon, for?' said she. Says I, 'Come go and see.' And she went with me. Next morning we went Down and found them well and ware glad to see us. Joseph talked with us about his translating and some revelations he had Received and from that time my wife Began to Beleve and Continuwed a full Believer until she Died" (BYU Studies, Autumn 1976, pp. 32–36).

Soon afterwards, Joseph Smith and Oliver Cowdery went to visit Mr. Knight, asking for additional help. Consequently, he bought "a Barral of Mackrel and some lined paper for writing . . . nine or ten Bushels of grain and five or six Bushels taters [potatoes] and a pound of tea, and I went Down to see him and they ware in want. Joseph and Oliver were gone to see if they Could find a place to work for provisions, But found none. They returned home and found me there with provisions, and they ware glad for they ware out" (BYU Studies, Autumn 1976, p. 36). With this help, the Prophet was able to finish the translation.

When Oliver Cowdery went to Pennsylvania to meet Joseph Smith, he stopped to see his friends, the Peter Whitmer, Sr., family, promising to send his impressions of the Prophet. He wrote them soon afterwards that "Joseph had told him his (Oliver's) secret thoughts, and all he had meditated about going to see him, which no man on earth knew, as he supposed, but himself" (*Millennial Star*, 9 Dec. 1878, p. 772). The Prophet at this time was being pressured by increasing mob threats to move from Harmony, Pennsylvania. Fortunately, he found refuge and a warm welcome with Oliver's friends, the Whitmers, in Fayette, New York, where he completed the translation of the Book of Mormon and received three revelations, Doctrine and Covenants 14–16, for members of the Whitmer family, during June 1829.

David Whitmer described how he personally assisted the Prophet during the final weeks of the translation. "Joseph sent for me . . . to come to Harmony to get him and Oliver and bring them to my father's house. I did not know what to do, I was pressed with my work. I had some 20 acres to plow, so I concluded I would finish plowing and then go. I got up one morning to go to work as usual, and on going to the field, found between five and seven acres of my ground had been plowed during the night.

"I don't know who did it; but it was done just as I would have done it myself, and the plow was left standing in the furrow.

"This enabled me to start sooner. When I arrived at Harmony, Joseph and Oliver were coming toward me, and met me some distance from the house. Oliver told me that Joseph had informed him when I started from home, where I had stopped the first night, how I read the sign at the tavern, where I stopped the next night, etc., and that I would be there that day before dinner, and this was why they had come out to meet me; all of which was exactly as Joseph had told Oliver, at which I was greatly astonished. When I was returning to Fayette, with Joseph and Oliver, all of us riding in the wagon, Oliver and I on an oldfashioned wooden spring seat and Joseph behind us; while traveling along in a clear open place, a very pleasant, nice-looking old man suddenly appeared by the side of our wagon and saluted us with, 'good morning, it is very warm,' at the same time wiping his face or forehead with his hand. We returned the salutation, and, by a sign from Joseph, I invited him to ride if he was going our way. But he said very pleasantly, 'No, I am going to Cumorah.' This name was something new to me, I did not know what Cumorah meant. We all gazed at him and at each other, and as I looked around enquiringly of Joseph, the old man instantly disappeared, so that I did not see him again. . . .

" . . . he had on his back a sort of knapsack with something in, shaped like a book. It was the messenger who had the plates, who had taken them from Joseph just prior to our starting from Harmony. Soon after our arrival home, I saw something which led me to the belief that the plates were placed or concealed in my father's barn. I frankly asked Joseph if my supposition was right, and he told me it was. Sometime after this, my mother was going to milk the cows, when she was met out near the yard by the same old man (judging by her description of him) who said to her: 'You have been very faithful and diligent in your labors, but you are tired because of the increase of your toil; it is proper therefore that you should receive a witness that your faith may be strengthened.' Thereupon he showed her the plates. My father and mother had a large family of their own, the addition to it therefore of Joseph, his wife Emma and Oliver very greatly increased the toil and anxiety of my mother. And although she had never complained she had sometimes felt that her labor was too much, or at least she was perhaps beginning to feel so. This circumstance, however, completely removed all such feelings and nerved her up for her increased responsibilities" (*Millennial Star*, 9 Dec. 1878, pp. 772–73).

4

THE RESTORATION OF
THE PRIESTHOOD

Doctrine and Covenants 13; 18

Joseph Smith and Oliver Cowdery's claim to ordination by an angel is unique in the annals of Christianity.

THE AARONIC AND MELCHIZEDEK
PRIESTHOODS RESTORED

While Joseph and Oliver were translating the Book of Mormon, they pondered a question regarding authority to baptize. Retiring to the woods near the Susquehanna River, they knelt in prayer. The heavens were opened; John the Baptist appeared, laid his hands upon their heads, and conferred upon them the Aaronic Priesthood. The prayer offered by this resurrected being on 15 May 1829, is recorded in Doctrine and Covenants 13. Both Joseph and Oliver testified to what they saw, heard, and physically felt as John placed his hands upon their heads. Each published accounts of the ordination, including the prayer uttered by John the Baptist (see Joseph Smith—History 1:68–74 and the note on pages 58–59 of the Pearl of Great Price).

Oliver wrote yet another testimony of this vision in a book of blessings while he was serving as recorder for the Church's Patriarch: "Our souls were drawn out in mighty prayer, to know how we might obtain the blessings of baptism and of the Holy Spirit according to the order of God; and we diligently sought for the right of the fathers, and the authority of the holy priesthood, and the power to administer the same; for we desired to be followers of righteousness, and in the possession of greater knowledge, even the knowledge of the mysteries of the kingdom of God. Therefore we repaired to the woods . . . and called upon the name of the Lord, and he answered us out of the heavens. And while we were in the heavenly vision, the angel came down and bestowed upon us this priesthood; and then, as I have said, we repaired to the water and were baptized. After this, we received the high and holy priesthood; but an account of this will be given elsewhere, or in another place" (*Improvement Era*, Oct. 1904, p. 942). John the Baptist informed Joseph and Oliver that "he acted under the direction of Peter, James and John, who held the keys of the Priesthood of Melchizedek, which Priesthood, he said, would in due time be conferred on us" (Joseph Smith–History 1:72). Although there is no record of the precise date on which the Melchizedek Priesthood was restored, two references in the Doctrine and Covenants confirm that Peter, James, and John restored this authority (see D&C 27:12; 128:20). The latter revelation indicates that the Melchizedek Priesthood was restored in the wilderness between Harmony, Pennsylvania, and Colesville, New York—probably about the time Joseph and Oliver moved to the Whitmer home in Fayette. Not long afterwards, the Prophet and some of his associates gathered "in the chamber of Mr. Whitmer's house" and prayed to know when they could exercise this higher power. "We had not long been engaged in solemn and fervent prayer," the Prophet recorded, "when the word of the Lord came unto us in the chamber [see D&C 128:21], commanding us that I should ordain Oliver Cowdery to be an Elder in the Church of Jesus Christ; and that he also should ordain me to the same office; and then to ordain others, as it should be made known unto us from time to time. We were, however, commanded to defer this our ordination until such times as it should be practicable to have our brethren, who had been and who should be baptized, assembled together, when we must have their sanction to our thus proceeding to ordain each other, and have them decide by vote whether they were willing to accept us as spiritual teachers or not" (*History of the Church*, 1:60–61).

During this gathering in the Whitmer home in June 1829, the Lord revealed Doctrine and Covenants 18. Many regard the Lord's statement in verse 9 of that section as evidence that the Melchizedek Priesthood had already been restored. The Lord's instruction to ordain brethren to a specific office in this priesthood would be carried out 6 April 1830 at the time of the official organization of the Church.

OLIVER COWDERY MAINTAINS HIS TESTIMONY

In 1848, many years after his apostasy, Oliver Cowdery returned to the Church. At a conference of the Saints in Iowa, Oliver bore witness of having been present during the restoration of the lesser and higher priesthoods. After describing his role as a scribe in the coming forth of the Book of Mormon, he said (as recorded by Reuben Miller): "I was present with Joseph when an holy angel from God came down from heaven and conferred on us or restored the lesser or Aaronic Priesthood, and said to us, at the same time, that it should remain upon the earth while the earth stands. I was also present with Joseph when the higher or Melchisedek Priesthood was conferred by the holy angel[s] from on high. This Priesthood was then conferred on each other, by the will and commandment of God. This Priesthood, as was then declared, is also to remain upon the earth until the last remnant of time. This holy priesthood or authority we then conferred upon many, and is just as good and valid as though God had done it in person. I laid my hands upon that man — yes, I laid my right hand upon his head (pointing to brother Hyde), and I conferred upon him this Priesthood, and he holds that Priesthood now. He was also called through me, by the prayer of faith, an Apostle of the Lord Jesus Christ" (*Millennial Star,* 20 Aug. 1859, p. 544). Shortly afterwards, the High Council authorized Oliver's rebaptism.

Another contemporary who reported Oliver Cowdery's testimony at the time of his return was Elder George A. Smith, an apostle and an early Church Historian: "He bore testimony in the most positive terms of the truth of the Book of Mormon — the restoration of the priesthood to the earth, and the mission of Joseph Smith as the Prophet of the last days; and told the people if they wanted to follow the right path, to keep the main channel of the stream — where the body of the Church goes, there is the authority; and all these lo here's and lo there's, have no authority; but this people have the true and holy priesthood; 'for the angel said unto Joseph Smith, jun., in my hearing, that this priesthood shall remain on the earth unto the end.' His testimony produced quite a sensation among the gentlemen present, who did not belong to the church, and it was gratefully received by all the Saints" (*Millennial Star,* 1 Feb. 1849, p. 14).

5

THE BOOK OF MORMON IS PUBLISHED AND THE CHURCH ORGANIZED

Doctrine and Covenants 17; 19–23

On several occasions during the early months of 1829 the Lord promised that "a marvelous work and a wonder [was] about to come forth among the children of men" (D&C 4:1; 6:1). This promise was fulfilled by two developments culminating in the spring of the following year: publication of the Book of Mormon and organization of the Church.

WITNESSES TO THE BOOK OF MORMON

Learning of prophecies in the Book of Mormon, three of Joseph Smith's close associates, Oliver Cowdery, David Whitmer, and Martin Harris, requested that Joseph inquire of the Lord to "know if they might not obtain of him the privilege to be these three special witnesses" mentioned in that work. "Finally," Joseph wrote, "they became so very solicitous, and urged me so much to inquire that at length I complied; and through the Urim and Thummim, I obtained of the Lord for them the following [D&C 17]" (*History of the Church,* 1:53). Each of the three had previously been promised that he might stand as a witness to the truth of the work in which he was engaged (see D&C 5:11–12, 24; 6:27–28; 8:1; 14:8).

Consequently, these three men, together with Joseph Smith, retired to the woods near Peter Whitmer's farmhouse in Fayette, New York. The vision that followed is one of the best documented manifestations in religious history. The testimony of the three, recorded shortly after the event, appeared in many early American newspapers. Their testimony was published in the first (1830) and in all subsequent editions of the Book of Mormon. Although all three of the witnesses left the Church (two later returned), not one ever denied his testimony. All three were interviewed on numerous occasions and reaffirmed their witness on their deathbed.

David Whitmer, the only witness who did not return to the Church, gave a detailed description of their experience:

"It was in June, 1829 — the latter part of the month, and the eight witnesses saw them, I think, the next day or the day after (i.e. one or two days after). Joseph showed them the plates himself, but the angel showed us (the three witnesses) the plates, as I suppose to fulfill the words of the book itself. Martin Harris was not with us at this time; he obtained a view of them afterwards, (the same day). Joseph, Oliver and myself were together when I saw them. We not only saw the plates of the Book of Mormon but also the brass plates, the plates of the Book of Ether, the plates containing the records of the wickedness and secret combinations of the people of the world down to the time of their being engraved, and many other plates. The fact is, it was just as though Joseph, Oliver and I were sitting just here on a log, when we were overshadowed by a light. It was not like the light of the sun nor like that of a fire, but more glorious and beautiful. It extended away round us, I cannot tell how far, but in the midst of this light about as far off as he sits (pointing to John C. Whitmer, sitting a few feet from him), there appeared as it were, a table with many records or plates upon it, besides the plates of the Book of Mormon, also the Sword of Laban, the directors — i.e., the ball which Lehi had — and the Interpreters. I saw them just as plain as I see this bed (striking the bed beside him with his hand), and I heard the voice of the Lord, as distinctly as I ever heard anything in my life, declaring that the records of the plates of the Book of Mormon were translated by the gift and power of God.

"Elder O. P. [Orson Pratt asked:] Did you see the angel at this time?

"D. W. Yes; he stood before us. Our testimony as recorded in the Book of Mormon is strictly and absolutely true, just as it is there written" (Millennial Star, 9 Dec. 1878, pp. 771–72).

That Oliver maintained his witness to the end of his life was confirmed by his wife, Elizabeth Ann Whitmer Cowdery, in a letter she wrote to her brother dated 8 March 1887: "Dear Brother David: — I, Elizabeth Cowdery, wife of Oliver Cowdery, do make the following statements: That my husband, Oliver Cowdery, bore his testimony to the truth and divine origin of the Book of Mormon, as one of the three witnesses of the Book of Mormon. . . . He always without one doubt or shudder of turning affirmed the divinity and truth of the Book of Mormon. 'God's promises naver fail' " (*The Return,* Dec. 1892, p. 7).

David Whitmer further confirmed that throughout their lives all three of these witnesses testified to the divine authenticity of the Book of Mormon: "I also testify to the world, that neither Oliver Cowdery or Martin Harris ever at any time denied their testimony. They both died reaffirming the truth of the divine authenticity of the Book of Mormon. I was present at the death bed of Oliver Cowdery, and his last words were, 'Brother David, be true to your testimony to the Book of Mormon.' He died here in Richmond, Mo., on March 3d, 1850. Many witnesses yet live in Richmond, who will testify to the truth of these facts, as well as to the good character of Oliver Cowdery" (*Address,* p. 8).

PUBLICATION OF THE BOOK OF MORMON

During the summer of 1829, Egbert B. Grandin had agreed to publish five thousand copies of the Book of Mormon for three thousand dollars. To assure payment, on 5 August 1829, Martin Harris mortgaged 240 acres of his farm to Mr. Grandin. According to the terms of this agreement, Harris was to pay the three thousand dollars within eighteen months. Should Harris default, Grandin was authorized to sell Martin's land at public auction to pay the debt. When the mortgage was negotiated, Martin Harris and others anticipated no difficulty in paying it off, assuming that receipts from Book of Mormon sales would be sufficient to meet the obligation. But opposition to "The Gold Bible" increased while the book was at the press. Lucy Mack Smith, the Prophet's mother, wrote: "When the inhabitants of the surrounding country perceived that the work still progressed, they became uneasy, and again called a large meeting. At this time, they gathered their forces together, far and near, and organizing themselves into a committee of the whole, they resolved, as before, never to purchase one of our books, when they should be printed. They then appointed a committee to wait upon E. B. Grandin, and inform him of the resolutions which they had passed, and also to explain to him the evil consequences which would result to him therefrom. The men who were appointed to do this errand, fulfilled their mission to the letter, and urged upon Mr. Grandin the necessity of his putting a stop to the printing, as the Smiths had lost all their property, and consequently would be unable to pay him for his work, except by the sale of the books. And this they would never be able to do, for the people would not purchase them. This information caused Mr. Grandin to stop printing, and we were again compelled to send for Joseph [who was then in Pennsylvania]. These trips, back and forth, exhausted nearly all our means, yet they seemed unavoidable.

"When Joseph came, he went immediately with Martin Harris to Grandin, and succeeded in removing his fears, so that he went on with the work, until the books were printed, which was in the spring of eighteen hundred and thirty" (History, pp. 166–67).

These events are the setting for Doctrine and Covenants 19. Martin was apparently concerned that he might lose his farm if this boycott against the Book of Mormon continued. The Lord admonished him not to covet his property and to give up a portion of it, if necessary, to pay the debt (D&C 19:26, 34–35). At great personal sacrifice, Martin Harris kept the Lord's command. Eventually, in April 1831, he sold 151 acres of his inheritance at public auction (Gunnell, "Martin Harris," pp. 37–38).

ORGANIZATION OF THE CHURCH

Doctrine and Covenants 20 through 23 were given in connection with the organization of the Church on 6 April 1830. Section 20 resulted from revelations received by the Prophet during preceding months, some perhaps received in late 1829. Section 20 declared the basic beliefs of the Church and described Church government and ordinances. Most of this revelation was available for discussion on the day the Church was organized in Peter Whitmer's farmhouse in Fayette, New York.

The Prophet included in his history a description of the events leading up to and transpiring on the day the Church was organized:

"In this manner did the Lord continue to give us instructions from time to time, concerning the duties which now devolved upon us; and among many other things of the kind, we obtained of Him the following, by the spirit of prophecy and revelation; which not only gave us much information, but also pointed out to us the precise day upon which, according to His will and commandment, we should proceed to organize His Church once more here upon the earth" (History of the Church, 1:64).

"Accordingly we met together for that purpose, at the house of Mr. Peter Whitmer, Sen., (being six in number,) on Tuesday, the sixth day of April, A.D., one thousand eight hundred and thirty. Having opened the meeting by solemn prayer to our Heavenly Father, we proceeded, according to previous commandment [revelation at the Whitmer home discussed in the previous chapter], to call on our brethren to know whether they accepted us as their teachers in the things of the Kingdom of God, and whether they were satisfied that we should proceed and be organized as a Church according to said commandment which we had received. To these several propositions they consented by a unanimous vote. I then laid my hands upon Oliver Cowdery, and ordained him an Elder of the 'Church of Jesus Christ of Latter-day Saints;' after which, he ordained me also to the office of an Elder of said Church. We then took bread, blessed it, and brake it with them; also wine, blessed it, and drank it with them. We then laid our hands on each individual member of the Church present, that they might receive the gift of the Holy Ghost, and be confirmed members of the Church of Christ. The Holy Ghost was poured out upon us to a very great degree—some prophesied, whilst we all praised the Lord, and rejoiced exceedingly. Whilst yet together, I received the following commandment: [D&C 21]" (*History of the Church*, 1:75–78).

Joseph Knight recalled that those present "all kneeld down and prayed and Joseph gave them instructions [on] how to Bild up the Church and exorted them to Be faithfull in all things for this is the work of God" (*BYU Studies*, Autumn 1976, p. 37).

The Prophet recorded: "After a happy time spent in witnessing and feeling for ourselves the powers and blessings of the Holy Ghost, through the grace of God bestowed upon us, we dismissed with the pleasing knowledge that we were now individually members of, and acknowledged of God, 'The Church of Jesus Christ,' organized in accordance with commandments and revelations given by Him to ourselves in these last days, as well as according to the order of the Church as recorded in the New Testament. Several persons who had attended the above meeting, became convinced of the truth and came forward shortly after, and were received into the Church; among the rest, my own father and mother were baptized, to my great joy and consolation; and about the same time, Martin Harris and Orrin Porter Rockwell" (*History of the Church*, 1:79).

Lucy Smith wrote that when her husband "came out of the water, Joseph stood upon the shore, and taking his father by the hand, he exclaimed, with tears of joy, 'Praise to my God! that I lived to see

my own father baptized into the true Church of Jesus Christ!' "
(*History*, p. 168).

At this time, when some believers who had been baptized in
other churches asked whether or not they needed to be baptized
again, Joseph received Doctrine and Covenants 22 for them. On the
same day the Church was organized, five converts expressed a desire
to know their respective duties. The Prophet inquired of the Lord
and received the revelations in Section 23. These were printed as
five separate chapters in the Book of Commandments and were all
dated 6 April 1830.

At the Church's first conference held at the Whitmer home on
9 June 1830, the material in Doctrine and Covenants 20 and 22
was accepted as authoritative. The minutes of the meeting record:
"Articles and Covenants read by Joseph Smith jr. and received by
unanimous voice of the whole congregation" (*Far West Record*, p.
1). This document was read at many early conferences, copied by
many Saints, and became a guide for proper belief and procedures
for the early Church.

6

ENCOURAGEMENT AND INSTRUCTION

Doctrine and Covenants 24–27

The months following the organization of the Church witnessed remarkable miracles and substantial growth. But persecution also increased, and it became so intense that some leaders had to seek safety in partial seclusion. Doctrine and Covenants 24 through 27 were given during this time to strengthen, encourage, and instruct early converts.

NEWEL KNIGHT AND THE CHURCH'S FIRST MIRACLE

Soon after the Church was organized in April 1830, Joseph Smith returned from Fayette, New York, to his home in Harmony, Pennsylvania. During the same month, Joseph went to visit the Knight family in nearby Colesville, New York. The Prophet's history records that he conversed on religious subjects with many people but especially with Joseph Knight's son Newel. "He and I had many serious conversations on the important subject of man's eternal salvation. We had got into the habit of praying much at our meetings." One morning Newel "retired into the woods; where, according to his own account afterwards, he made several attempts to pray, but could scarcely do so, feeling that he had not done his duty, in refusing to pray in the presence of others. He began to feel uneasy, and continued to feel worse both in mind and body, until, upon reaching his own house, his appearance was such as to alarm his wife very much. He requested her to go and bring me to him. I went and found him suffering very much in his mind, and his body acted upon in a very strange manner; his visage and limbs distorted and twisted in every shape and appearance possible to imagine; and finally he was caught up off the floor of the apartment, and tossed about most fearfully.

". . . I succeeded in getting hold of him by the hand, when almost immediately he spoke to me, and with great earnestness requested me to cast the devil out of him, saying that he knew he was in him, and that he also knew that I could cast him out.

"I replied, 'If you know that I can, it shall be done;' and then almost unconsciously I rebuked the devil, and commanded him in the name of Jesus Christ to depart from him; when immediately Newel spoke out and said that he saw the devil leave him and vanish from his sight. This was the first miracle which was done in the Church. . . .

"This scene was now entirely changed, for as soon as the devil had departed from our friend, his countenance became natural, his distortions of body ceased, and almost immediately the Spirit of the Lord descended upon him, and the visions of eternity were opened to his view. . . . He afterwards related his experience as follows:

" 'I now began to feel a most pleasing sensation resting on me, and immediately the visions of heaven were opened to my view. I felt myself attracted upward, and remained for some time enwrapt in contemplation, insomuch that I knew not what was going on in the room. By and by, I felt some weight pressing upon my shoulder and the side of my head, which served to recall me to a sense of my situation, and I found that the Spirit of the Lord had actually caught me up off the floor, and that my shoulder and head were pressing against the beams.'

"All this was witnessed by many, to their great astonishment and satisfaction, when they saw the devil thus cast out, and the power of God, and His Holy Spirit thus made manifest. As may be expected, such a scene as this contributed much to make believers of those who witnessed it, and finally the greater part of them became members of the Church" (*History of the Church*, 1:82–84).

Concerning subsequent events Newel Knight wrote: "During the last week in May [1830] I went on a visit to Fayette and was baptized by David Whitmer.

"On the [ninth] day of June, 1830, the first conference was held by the Church. Our number consisted of about thirty, besides many others who came to learn of our principles, or were already believers, but had not been baptized. Having opened the meeting by singing and prayer, we partook of the emblems of the body and blood of our Lord Jesus Christ. A number were confirmed who had lately been baptized, and several were called and ordained to various offices in the Priesthood. Much good instruction was given, and the Holy Ghost was poured out upon us in a marvelous manner. Many prophesied, while others had the heavens opened to their view. It was a scene long to be remembered" (*Classic Experiences*, p. 52).

OPPOSITION INCREASES

Newel Knight's account sheds light on the type of persecution the Saints were suffering at Colesville: "Soon after conference Joseph Smith the Prophet, accompanied by his wife, Oliver Cowdery, John Whitmer and David Whitmer, came to Colesville to make us a visit. There were many in our neighborhood who believed, and were anxiously waiting for an opportunity to be baptized. Meeting was appointed for the Sabbath, and on Saturday afternoon we erected a dam across a stream which was close by, with the intention of baptizing those who applied on Sunday, but during the night a mob collected and tore away the dam. This prevented us from attending to the ordinance of baptism that day." Nevertheless, on Sunday "we held our meeting, Oliver Cowdery preached, others bore testimony to the Book of Mormon, the doctrine of repentance, baptism for the remission of sins, and the laying on of hands for the gift of the Holy Ghost, etc. In the audience were those who had torn down the dam. They seemed desirous of giving us trouble, but did not until after the meeting was dismissed, when they immediately commenced talking to those whom they considered our friends, to try to turn them against us and our doctrine. . . .

"Early on Monday morning we were on the alert, and before our enemies were aware of it, Oliver Cowdery proceeded to baptize . . . but before the baptism was entirely finished, the mob began to collect again. We retired to my father's house, and the mob, which numbered about fifty surrounded the house, raging with anger, and apparently wishing to commit violence against us. So violent and troublesome were they, that the brethren were obliged to leave my father's house and they succeeded in reaching mine. The mob who soon found where they had gone, followed them and it was only by great prudence on our part and help from our Heavenly Father that they were kept from laying violent hands upon us.

"A meeting had been appointed for the evening to confirm those who had been baptized in the morning. The time appointed had arrived, and our friends had nearly all collected together, when, to our great surprise and sorrow, the constable came and arrested Brother Joseph Smith, Jun., on a warrant charging him with being a disorderly person, and of setting the country in an uproar, by preaching the Book of Mormon. The constable soon after he had arrested Joseph, told him that the plan of those who had got out the warrant for his arrest, was to get him into the hands of the mob who were now lying in ambush for him, and that he, the constable, was determined to save Joseph from them, as he found him to be a different person to what he had been represented. This proved true, for they had not proceeded far from the house, when the wagon in which Joseph and the constable were riding, was surrounded by the mob, who seemed only to await some signal from the constable, but to their great discomfiture, he gave the horses the whip and was soon out of their reach. As the constable was driving briskly along, one of the wagon wheels came off, which accident left them almost in the hands of the mob, who had pursued them closely. But the constable was an expert man and managed to get the wheel on again, before the mob overtook him, and soon left them in the rear once more.

"He drove on to the town of South Bainbridge, Chenango county, where he lodged Joseph in an upper room of a tavern; and in order that all might be safe for himself and Joseph, he slept, or laid during the night with his feet against the door, and kept a loaded gun by him, (Joseph occupied a bed in the same room) and declared that if they were unlawfully molested he would fight for Joseph, and defend him to the utmost of his ability.

"On the following day a court was convened for the purpose of investigating the charges which had been made against Joseph Smith, Jun. On account of the many scandalous reports which had been put in circulation, a great excitement prevailed. . . .

". . . His persecutors managed to detain the court until they had succeeded in obtaining a warrant from Broome county. This warrant they served upon him at the very moment he had been acquitted by the court.

"The constable who served this second warrant upon Joseph had no sooner arrested him, than he began to abuse him; and so heartless was he, that, although Joseph had been kept all day in court without anything to eat since the morning, he hurried him off to Broome County, a distance of about fifteen miles, before allowing him to eat. The constable took him to a tavern, where were gathered a number of men, who used every means to abuse, ridicule, and insult him. They spit upon him, pointed their fingers at him, saying,

'Prophesy! prophesy!' and used their utmost ability to pain and torment his mind; and thus did they imitate those who crucified the Savior of mankind, not knowing what they did. . . . Next day he was brought before the magistrate's court of Colesville, Broome county, and placed on trial. . . .

"They proceeded for a considerable time in [a] frivolous and vexatious manner, when finally I was called upon. . . .

"As soon as I had been sworn, Mr. Seymour proceeded to interrogate me as follows:

"Question. – 'Did the prisoner, Joseph Smith, Jun., cast the devil out of you?'

"Answer. – 'No, sir.'

"Q. – 'Why, have you not had the devil cast out of you?'

"A. – 'Yes, sir.'

"Q. – 'And had not Joseph Smith some hand in it being done?

"A. – 'Yes, sir.'

"Q. – 'And did he not cast him out of you?'

"A. – 'No, sir, it was done by the power of God, and Joseph Smith was the instrument in the hands of God on this occasion. He commanded him to come out of me in the name of Jesus Christ.'

"Q. – 'And are you sure it was the devil?'

"A. – 'Yes, sir.'

"Q. – 'Did you see him after he was cast out of you?'

"A. – 'Yes, sir, I saw him.' "

"Q. – 'Pray, what did he look like?'

(Here one of the lawyers on the part of the defense told me I need not answer that question). I replied:

" 'I believe, I need not answer you that question, but I will do it if I am allowed to ask you one, and you can answer it. Do you, Mr. Seymour, understand the things of the Spirit?'

" 'No,' answered Mr. Seymour, 'I do not pretend to such big things.'

" 'Well, then,' I replied, 'it will be of no use for me to tell you what the devil looked like, for it was a spiritual sight and spiritually discerned, and, of course, you would not understand it were I to tell you of it.'

"The lawyer dropped his head, while the loud laugh of the audience proclaimed his discomfiture. . . .

"After all the efforts of the people and court to sustain the charges brought against Joseph proving an entire failure, he was discharged and succeeded in making good his escape from the mob through the instrumentality of his new friend, the constable" (*Classic Experiences*, pp. 53–61).

Joseph visited the Knight family once again before leaving the region. A few hours before his arrival, Newel's wife had a dream that enabled her to know that the Prophet would visit them. Joseph declared, "Our faith [was] much strengthened concerning dreams and visions in the last days, foretold by the ancient Prophet Joel; and although we this time were forced to seek safety from our enemies by flight, yet did we feel confident that eventually we should come off victorious, if we only continued faithful to Him who had called us forth from darkness into the marvelous light of the everlasting Gospel of our Lord Jesus Christ" (*History of the Church*, 1:101).

Shortly after returning to his home in Harmony, Pennsylvania, the Prophet received three revelations, instructing him how to proceed in leading the Church. Joseph was instructed in Doctrine and Covenants 24 to devote his full time to strengthening Church branches in the face of growing opposition. Doctrine and Covenants 25 was given for the Prophet's wife, Emma. It had been difficult for her to understand why she couldn't have the reassurance that could come through seeing the plates, which had already been shown to several others. This revelation sought to give her needed comfort and direction.

Newel Knight described the setting of Doctrine and Covenants 26, another far-reaching revelation given August 1830: "In the beginning of August I, in company with my wife, went to make a visit to Brother Joseph Smith, Jun., who then resided at Harmony, Penn. We found him and his wife well, and in good spirits. We had a happy meeting. It truly gave me joy to again behold his face. As neither Emma, the wife of Joseph Smith, nor my wife had been confirmed, we concluded to attend to that holy ordinance at this time, and also to partake of the sacrament, before we should leave for home. In order to prepare for this, Brother Joseph set out to procure some wine for the occasion, but he had gone only a short distance, when he was met by a heavenly messenger, and received [a] revelation [see D&C 27]. . . .

"In obedience to this revelation we prepared some wine of our own make, and held our meeting, consisting of only five persons namely, Joseph Smith and wife, John Whitmer, and myself and wife.

We partook of the sacrament, after which we confirmed the two sisters into the Church, and spent the evening in a glorious manner. The Spirit of the Lord was poured out upon us. We praised the God of Israel and rejoiced exceedingly" (*Classic Experiences*, pp. 62–63; see also *History of the Church*, 1:106).

7

MISSION TO THE LAMANITES

Doctrine and Covenants 28; 30; 32

In September 1830 Oliver Cowdery was called to preach the gospel to the Lamanites (D&C 28:8). Shortly thereafter, Peter Whitmer, Jr. (D&C 30:5), Parley P. Pratt, and Ziba Peterson were instructed to accompany him (D&C 32:1–3). The great significance of this mission would not be among native Americans, but it would be the means of bringing many non-Indians into the Church. It would also give the Latter-day Saints their first contact with two areas of future importance: Kirtland, Ohio, and Independence, Missouri.

Only a few months before his calling as a missionary, Parley P. Pratt learned of the restored gospel while preaching the need to re-establish the ancient Christian order. He recalled that an old Baptist deacon by the name of Hamlin told him about a book, "a STRANGE BOOK, a VERY STRANGE BOOK!" that he had in his possession, which had just been published. "I inquired of him how or where the book was to be obtained," he continued. "He promised me the perusal of it, at his house the next day, if I would call. I felt a strange interest in the book. . . . Next morning I called at his house, where, for the first time, my eyes beheld the 'BOOK OF MORMON.' . . .

"I opened it with eagerness, and read its title page. I then read the testimony of several witnesses in relation to the manner of its being found and translated. After this I commenced its contents by course. I read all day; eating was a burden, I had no desire for food; sleep was a burden when the night came, for I preferred reading to sleep.

"As I read, the spirit of the Lord was upon me, and I knew and comprehended that the book was true, as plainly and manifestly as a man comprehends and knows that he exists" (*Autobiography*, pp. 36–37). After his conversion, he led his fellow missionaries to northeastern Ohio, where he knew people who were seeking religious truth.

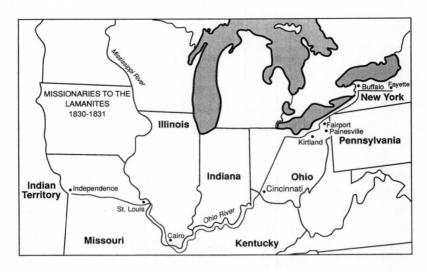

CONVERSIONS IN KIRTLAND

Parley P. Pratt has provided the most complete account of the mission to the Lamanites. Leaving his wife and children at the log cabin of Peter Whitmer, Parley and the other missionaries started westward on foot in the latter part of October 1830. After traveling about two hundred miles, they arrived in Mentor, Ohio, at the home of Parley's friend, Sidney Rigdon, an influential restorationist preacher. "He received us cordially and entertained us with hospitality," Parley recalled. "We soon presented him with a Book of Mormon, and related to him the history of the same. He was much interested, and promised a thorough perusal of the book.

"We tarried in this region for some time, and devoted our time to the ministry, and visiting from house to house. . . .

"The news of our coming was soon noised abroad, and the news of the discovery of the Book of Mormon and the marvelous events connected with it. The interest and excitement now became general in Kirtland, and in all the region round about. The people thronged us night and day, insomuch that we had no time for rest and retirement. Meetings were convened in different neighborhoods, and multitudes came together soliciting our attendance; while thousands flocked about us daily; some to be taught, some for curiosity, some to obey the gospel, and some to dispute or resist it" (*Autobiography*, pp. 47–48).

Although the missionaries had arrived in Ohio carrying satchels filled with copies of the Book of Mormon, there were not enough copies for all who desired to read that record. Mary Rollins, a twelve-year-old girl living in Kirtland, borrowed a copy from Isaac Morley. She recorded: "If any person in this world was ever perfectly happy in the possession of any coveted treasure I was when I had permission to read that wonderful book. Uncle and Aunt were Methodists, so when I got into the house, I exclaimed, 'Oh, Uncle, I have got the "Golden Bible". ' Well, there was consternation in the house for a few moments, and I was severely reprimanded for being so presumtious as to ask such a favor, when Brother Morley had not read it himself. However, we all took turns reading it until very late in the night — as soon as it was light enough to see, I was up and learned the first verse in the book. When I reached Brother Morley's they had been up for only a little while. When I handed him the book, he remarked, 'I guess you did not read much in it.' I showed him how far we had read. He was surprised, and said, 'I don't believe you can tell me one word of it.' I then repeated the first verse, also the outlines of the history of Nephi. He gazed at me in surprise, and said, 'child, take this book home and finish it, I can wait' " (*Utah Genealogical and Historical Magazine,* July 1926, p. 194).

John Murdock, a farmer in that area, was converted in November 1830, also by reading the Book of Mormon. In one week he read the book, was baptized, confirmed, ordained an elder, and sent forth as a missionary to tell others of the reality of the Restoration.

Meanwhile, another restorationist, Philo Dibble, traveled to Kirtland to investigate the message being proclaimed by the missionaries. After listening to the elders, he received a witness by the Spirit that the gospel had been restored, and he was baptized on the same day.

By mid November 1830, Sidney Rigdon had resolved his doubts concerning modern scripture, latter-day revelation, and the elders' claim of restored authority. On Sunday, November 14, this Reformed Baptist preacher spoke to a large congregation in the Methodist meetinghouse in Kirtland, announcing his conversion to the restored Church. Shortly thereafter he and his wife were baptized by Oliver Cowdery and were overwhelmed with tears of joy.

Parley P. Pratt reported that in less than one month, the missionaries baptized in Kirtland and vicinity some 127 converts. After ordaining a few leaders to preside over the newly created branches, the missionaries to the Lamanites resumed their journey. Parley stopped in the area where he had lived when he was first married. There he found people who "wished to learn and obey the fulness of the gospel—were ready to entertain us and hear us preach. Others were filled with envy, rage and lying." He spent the night at the home of Simeon Carter and left a copy of the Book of Mormon with him. "He read it with attention. It wrought deeply upon his mind, and he went fifty miles to the church we had left in Kirtland, and was there baptized and ordained an Elder. He then returned to his home and commenced to preach and baptize. A church of about sixty members was soon organized" (*Autobiography*, pp. 48, 51).

PREACHING TO THE INDIANS
NEAR INDEPENDENCE, MISSOURI

After traveling by foot across the states of Ohio, Indiana, and Missouri, they reached what was then the western frontier of the United States. Crossing the Kansas River into Indian territory, they located a tribe of Delaware Indians. "We immediately inquired for the residence of the principal Chief," Parley wrote, "and were soon introduced to an aged and venerable looking man, who had long stood at the head of the Delawares, and been looked up to as the Great Grandfather, or Sachem of ten nations or tribes.

"He was seated on a sofa of furs, skins and blankets, before a fire in the center of his lodge; which was a comfortable cabin, consisting of two large rooms.

"His wives were neatly dressed, partly in calicoes and partly in skins; and wore a vast amount of silver ornaments. As we entered his cabin he took us by the hand with a hearty welcome, and then motioned us to be seated on a pleasant seat of blankets, or robes. His wives, at his bidding, set before us a tin pan full of beans and corn boiled up together, which proved to be good eating; although three of us made use alternately of the same wooden spoon.

"There was an interpreter present and through him we commenced to make known our errand, and to tell him of the Book of Mormon. We asked him to call the council of his nation together and give us a hearing in full. . . .

" . . . He despatched a messenger, and in about an hour had some forty men collected around us in his lodge, who, after shaking us by the hand, were seated in silence; and in a grave and dignified manner awaited the announcement of what we had to offer. The chief then requested us to proceed; or rather, begin where we began before, and to complete our communication. Elder Cowdery then commenced as follows:

" 'Aged Chief and Venerable Council of the Delaware nation; we are glad of this opportunity to address you as our red brethren and friends. We have travelled a long distance from towards the rising sun to bring you glad news; we have travelled the wilderness, crossed the deep and wide rivers, and waded in the deep snows, and in the face of the storms of winter, to communicate to you great knowledge which has lately come to our ears and hearts; and which will do the red man good as well as the pale face.

" 'Once the red men were many; they occupied the country from sea to sea—from the rising to the setting sun; the whole land was theirs; the Great Spirit gave it to them, and no pale faces dwelt among them. But now they are few in numbers; their possessions are small, and the pale faces are many.

" 'Thousands of moons ago, when the red men's forefathers dwelt in peace and possessed this whole land, the Great Spirit talked with them, and revealed His law and His will, and much knowledge to their wise men and prophets. This they wrote in a Book; together with their history, and the things which should befall their children in the latter days.

" 'This Book was written on plates of gold, and handed down from father to son for many ages and generations.

" 'It was then that the people prospered, and were strong and mighty; they cultivated the earth; built buildings and cities, and abounded in all good things, as the pale faces now do.

" 'But they became wicked; they killed one another and shed much blood; they killed their prophets and wise men, and sought to destroy the Book. The Great Spirit became angry, and would speak to them no more; they had no more good and wise dreams; no more visions; no more angels sent among them by the Great Spirit; and the Lord commanded Mormon and Moroni, their last wise men and prophets, to hide the Book in the earth, that it might be preserved in safety, and be found and made known in the latter day to the pale faces who should possess the land. . . . And if the red man would then receive this Book and learn the things written in it, and do according thereunto . . .

" 'Then should the red men become great, and have plenty to eat and good clothes to wear, and should be in favor with the Great Spirit and be his children' " (*Autobiography*, pp. 53–55).

After telling these people about the Prophet Joseph Smith and the coming forth of the Book of Mormon, they gave the chief a copy of the new witness for Christ.

"There was a pause in the council," Parley wrote, "and some conversation in their own tongue, after which the chief made the following reply:

" 'We feel truly thankful to our white friends who have come so far, and been at such pains to tell us good news, and especially this new news concerning the Book of our forefathers; it makes us glad in here'—placing his hand on his heart.

" 'It is now winter, we are new settlers in this place; the snow is deep, our cattle and horses are dying, our wigwams are poor; we have much to do in the spring—to build houses, and fence and make farms; but we will build a council house, and meet together, and you shall read to us and teach us more concerning the Book of our fathers and the will of the Great Spirit' " (*Autobiography*, pp. 56).

The missionaries continued to instruct the old chief and many of his tribe for several days:

"We found several among them who could read, and to them we gave copies of the Book, explaining to them that it was the Book of their forefathers.

"Some began to rejoice exceedingly, and took great pains to tell the news to others, in their own language.

"The excitement now reached the frontier settlements in Missouri, and stirred up the jealousy and envy of the Indian agents and sectarian missionaries to that degree that we were soon ordered out of the Indian country as disturbers of the peace; and even threatened with the military in case of non-compliance.

"We accordingly departed from the Indian country, . . . and commenced laboring in Jackson County, Missouri, among the whites. We were well received, and listened to by many; and some were baptized and added to the Church.

"Thus ended our first Indian Mission, in which we had preached the gospel in its fulness, and distributed the record of their forefathers among three tribes, viz: the Catteraugus Indians, near Buffalo, N. Y., the Wyandots of Ohio, and the Delawares west of Missouri.

"We trust that at some future day, when the servants of God go forth in power to the remnant of Joseph, some precious seed will be found growing in their hearts, which was sown by us in that early day" (*Autobiography*, p. 57).

8

FUTURE LEADERS SEEK GUIDANCE FROM THE LORD

Doctrine and Covenants 34–36

Many individuals who met the Prophet Joseph Smith asked him to inquire of the Lord concerning them. Several sections now in the Doctrine and Covenants were the result. During November and December 1830, while living with the Whitmer family in Fayette, the Prophet received four revelations directed to three converts: Orson Pratt, Sidney Rigdon, and Edward Partridge.

ORSON PRATT

Speaking through the Prophet, the Lord told Orson Pratt he was to prepare for the Second Coming by preaching the gospel "as with the sound of a trump, both long and loud" (D&C 34:5–6). Orson would become one of the most successful missionaries and influential members of the Quorum of the Twelve in the history of the Church. He summarized his conversion and the events that led to his meeting with the Prophet:

"From the age of ten to nineteen I saw much of the world, and was tossed about without any permanent abiding place; but through the grace of God, I was kept from many of the evils to which young people are exposed; the early impressions of morality and religion, instilled into my mind by my parents, always remained with me; and I often felt a great anxiety to be prepared for a future state; but never commenced, in real earnest, to seek after the Lord, until the autumn of 1829. I then began to pray very fervently, repenting of every sin. In the silent shades of night, while others were slumbering upon their pillows, I often retired to some secret place in the lonely fields or solitary wilderness, and bowed before the Lord, and prayed for hours with a broken heart and contrite spirit; this was my comfort and delight. The greatest desire of my heart was for the Lord to manifest His will concerning me. I continued to pray in this fervent manner until September, 1830, at which time two Elders of the Church of Jesus Christ of Latter-day Saints, came into the neighborhood, one of which was my brother Parley. They held several meetings which I attended.

"Being convinced of the divine authenticity of the doctrine they taught, I was baptized September 19, 1830. This was my birthday, being nineteen years old. I was the only person in the country who received and obeyed the message. Shortly after my baptism the Elders left.

"In October, 1830, I traveled westward over two hundred miles to see Joseph Smith, the Prophet. I found him in Fayette, Seneca County, N. Y., residing at the house of Mr. [Peter] Whitmer. I soon became intimately acquainted with this good man, and also with the witnesses of the Book of Mormon. By my request, on the 4th of Nov., the Prophet Joseph inquired of the Lord for me, and received the revelation published in the Doctrine and Covenants [D&C 34].

"On the 1st day of December, 1830, I was confirmed and in accordance with the word of the Lord, I was ordained an Elder under the hands of the Prophet. My first mission was to Colesville, Broome County, N. Y., where I commenced to open my mouth in public meetings, and teach the things of God, as the Holy Ghost gave me utterance" (*Journals*, pp. 8–10).

SIDNEY RIGDON AND EDWARD PARTRIDGE

Before the missionaries to the Lamanites left Ohio, they called Sidney Rigdon to be a leader over the Saints. He recognized his need for assistance, because he had just been baptized and did not know many principles of belief or practice. He decided to travel east, find Joseph, and seek counsel. He was accompanied by one of his followers, Edward Partridge, a successful hatter in nearby Painesville, who was delaying his baptism until he had personally met Joseph and received a witness of the Prophet's divine calling. Lydia Partridge recalled that when her husband began the journey, he was not fully convinced of the truth of the gospel taught by the elders.

Because Edward Partridge was noted for his integrity, other "inquirers" awaited Edward's appraisal of Joseph Smith's character before making up their minds. (Backman, *Heavens Resound*, p. 40.) Meanwhile, Joseph Smith, Sr., had moved from Manchester to a home east of Waterloo, not far from Fayette, where the Church had been organized. Lucy Mack Smith described the events that occurred in her home when the two strangers from Ohio first met her son:

"In December [1830], Joseph appointed a meeting at our house. While he was preaching, Sidney Rigdon and Edward Partridge came in and seated themselves in the congregation. When Joseph had finished his discourse, he gave all who had any remarks to make, the privilege of speaking. Upon this, Mr. Partridge arose, and stated that he had been to Manchester, with the view of obtaining further information respecting the doctrine which we preached; but, not finding us, he had made some inquiry of our neighbors concerning our characters, which they stated had been unimpeachable, until Joseph deceived us [them] relative to the Book of Mormon. He also said that he had walked over our farm, and observed the good order and industry which it exhibited; and, having seen what we had sacrificed for the sake of our faith, and having heard that our veracity was not questioned upon any other point than that of our religion, he believed our testimony, and was ready to be baptized, 'if,' said he, 'Brother Joseph will baptize me.'

" 'You are now,' replied Joseph, 'much fatigued, brother Partridge, and you had better rest to-day, and be baptized tomorrow.'

" 'Just as Brother Joseph thinks best,' replied Mr. Partridge, 'I am ready at any time.'

"He was accordingly baptized the next day [11 December 1830]" (*History*, pp. 191–92).

The Prophet recorded that shortly after the arrival of Sidney Rigdon and Edward Partridge, the Lord spoke to him concerning them, giving the revelations that are now Doctrine and Covenants 35 and 36 (*History of the Church*, 1:128).

During the 1820s Sidney Rigdon had been influenced by the teachings of Alexander Campbell and was a successful restorationist preacher in Ohio, but when Campbell began organizing followers in 1830 in a movement that became the Disciples of Christ, Rigdon refused to unite with him. Unlike Campbell, Rigdon believed in a restoration of God's power and in the establishment of a communal order of living. Unlike the Latter-day Saints, Rigdon believed that the Bible was the sole standard of faith and that when individuals accepted Christ they were thereby endowed with God's authority without the need of special ordination. After listening to the Latter-day Saint missionaries, the former Baptist preacher recognized significant differences between the teachings of Alexander Campbell and Joseph Smith. Some of these differences were identified in the revelation recorded by the Prophet shortly after meeting Rigdon: "Behold thou wast sent forth, even as John," the revelation read, "to prepare the way before me." Before his conversion to Mormonism, the revelation continued, Rigdon "baptized by water unto repentance but they received not the Holy Ghost." After he had received God's authority, individuals who were baptized by him would "receive the Holy Ghost by the laying on of hands." This revelation further emphasized that "miracles, signs, and wonders" would be manifest among believers (D&C 35:4–9).

Three years later, Sidney Rigdon would be called as a "spokesman" for Joseph Smith and the Church (D&C 100:9). In that capacity, he published a series of articles in the *Latter Day Saints' Messenger and Advocate,* emphasizing differences between the "Restoration" as taught by the Prophet Joseph Smith and that taught by other faiths. He affirmed that the biblical prophecy regarding restitution of all things included a restoration of "all spiritual gifts" and "every blessing which had ever been enjoyed among men from the first to the last" (*Messenger and Advocate,* May 1835, p. 117). Rigdon added that Joseph Smith not only restored correct beliefs, such as the principle of the laying on of hands for the gift of the Holy Ghost, but also received God's power and authority. He further testified that this restored power included revelations, visions, healing, prophecy, and speaking in tongues.

Sidney Rigdon was also called by revelation to be a scribe in making what came to be known as the Joseph Smith Translation of the Bible (D&C 35:20, 23), restoring, clarifying and correcting the biblical text by inspiration—a work that began as early as June 1830. Immediately he began writing as the Prophet dictated to him, and he assisted the Prophet in recording the visions and prophecy of Enoch and other portions of the Old Testament. After the Saints moved to Ohio, Rigdon served as scribe for more of Joseph's translation of the New Testament than any other person.

Because of Rigdon's education, maturity, and eloquence as a speaker, early critics claimed that he was the dominant influence in the translation of the Bible and was the principal author of the Book of Mormon. Refuting these allegations, however, Sidney Rigdon emphatically reiterated his testimony. According to his son John, "My father . . . looked at me a moment and slowly raised his hand above his head and slowly said, with a tear glistening in his eyes: 'My son,

I can swear before high heaven that what I have told you about the origin of that book is true. Your mother and sister, Mrs. Athalia Robinson, were present when that book was handed to me in Mentor, Ohio, and all I ever knew about the origin of that book was what Parley P. Pratt, Oliver Cowdery, Joseph Smith, and the witnesses who claimed they saw the plates have told me, and in all of my intimacy with Joseph Smith, he never told me but the one story, and that was he found it engraved upon gold plates in a hill near Palmyra, NY, and that an angel had appeared to him and directed him where to find it, and I have never to you or anyone else told but [this] one story, and that I now repeat to you' " ("Life Story," pp. 193–94).

The Lord had made a distinction between the roles of Joseph, who was to "prophesy," and of Sidney, who was to call on the scriptures to prove the Prophet's words (D&C 35:23). Consequently, for many years, Sidney Rigdon, serving as first counselor in the First Presidency, used his knowledge of the scriptures to substantiate and promulgate the truths taught by the Prophet Joseph Smith.

In the revelation for Edward Partridge, the Lord admonished him to share his newfound faith (D&C 36). Edward Partridge returned to his home in Ohio at the beginning of February 1831 after two months' absence. "After his arrival home," Edward's daughter Emily wrote, "his old and most intimate friends that had been so anxious for him to go and find out the truth of the reports about 'Mormonism' because of his honesty and superior judgment, pronounced him crazy when he declared the Book of Mormon true" ("Autobiography," p. 6). Within a few days of his return from New York, Edward Partridge became the Church's first bishop (D&C 41:9). In this capacity he administered the law of consecration and assigned stewardships (see Chapter 10). Near the end of 1831, Bishop Partridge, representing the Church, purchased sixty-three acres of land at Independence, Missouri, including the spot where Joseph Smith had placed a cornerstone for the future temple. Just over a year and a half later, when mob violence commenced against the Saints in Jackson County, Missouri, Edward was one of two Latter-day Saints who were tarred and feathered. This incident occurred on the same day that the Saints' press and the nearly completed copies of the Book of Commandments were destroyed (see Chapter 1). Edward Partridge served faithfully as the Church's first presiding bishop until his death in 1840.

9

GATHERING IN OHIO

Doctrine and Covenants 37–38

The number of converts grew rapidly in Ohio after the visit by the missionaries sent to the Lamanites (see Chapter 7). By December 1830, there were more Church members in Ohio than in New York. While visiting Joseph Smith in New York, Sidney Rigdon informed him of the conversions in Ohio and invited him to go there. Joseph inquired of the Lord and received two revelations (D&C 37 at the end of 1830 and D&C 38 at the beginning of 1831), telling him and other Church members to migrate from New York and Pennsylvania to "the Ohio." This move was but the first step in the Church's westward migration. In Ohio, the Saints were to develop a strong nucleus from which the gospel and the Church might spread.

JOSEPH SMITH MOVES TO OHIO

The Saints in New York and Pennsylvania immediately began preparing to move to Ohio. Joseph Smith's mother recorded in her history that late in December 1830, "Joseph received a letter from John Whitmer, desiring his immediate assistance at Kirtland in regulating the affairs of the church there. Joseph inquired of the Lord, and received a commandment to go straightway to Kirtland with his family and effects." Consequently, the Prophet was the first to depart for Ohio. He and his wife traveled with Sidney Rigdon and Edward Partridge, who were returning to their homes near Kirtland. "When they were about starting," Lucy continued, "they preached at our house on Seneca River; and, on their way, they preached at the house of Calvin Stoddard, and likewise at the house of Preserved Harris [brother of Martin Harris]. At each of these places, they baptized several individuals into the Church" (*History*, pp. 192–93).

Joseph and his companions arrived in Kirtland about the first of February 1831. When the sleigh pulled up in front of a store owned by Sidney Gilbert and Newel Whitney, the Prophet sprang out, "walked into the store and to where the junior partner was standing. 'Newel K. Whitney! Thou art the man!' he exclaimed, extending his hand cordially, as if to an old and familiar acquaintance. 'You have the advantage of me,' replied the merchant, as he mechanically took the proffered hand, 'I could not call you by the name as you have me.' 'I am Joseph the Prophet,' said the stranger smiling. 'You've prayed me here, now what do you want of me?'" (*History of the Church*, 1:146 n.). The Whitneys kindly extended hospitality to the Prophet and his wife.

Other groups of Saints followed, and by the summer of 1831 about two hundred New York and Pennsylvania Saints had migrated to Ohio. Some of the challenges, trials, and unusual experiences that accompanied this migration were recorded by two participants, Newel Knight and Lucy Mack Smith.

NEWEL KNIGHT AND THE COLESVILLE BRANCH

Newel Knight described how the Saints received the revelation to move: "On the 2nd of January, 1831, the third conference of the Church assembled. . . .

"It was at this conference that we were instructed as a people, to begin the gathering of Israel, and a revelation was given to the prophet on this subject [D&C 38].

"Having returned home from conference, in obedience to the commandment which had been given, I, together with the Colesville Branch, began to make preparations to go to Ohio. . . .

"As might be expected, we were obliged to make great sacrifices of our property. The most of my time was occupied in visiting the brethren, and helping to arrange their affairs, so that we might travel together in one company. Having made the best arrangements we could for the journey, we bade adieu to all we held dear on this earth and in the early part of April started for our destination.

"We had proceeded but a few days on our journey, when I was subpoenaed as a witness, and had to go [back] to Colesville. On arriving there it was very evident that this plan had been adopted by our enemies to add a little more to the persecutions already heaped upon us. The whole company declined traveling until I should return.

"Soon after I left, my aunt, Electa Peck, fell and broke her shoulder in a most shocking manner; a surgeon was called to relieve her sufferings, which were very great. My aunt dreamed that I returned and laid my hands upon her, prayed for her, and she was made whole, and pursued her journey with the company. She related this dream to the surgeon who replied, 'If you are able to travel in many weeks it will be a miracle, and I will be a Mormon too.'

"I arrived at the place, where the company had stopped, late in the evening; but, on learning of the accident, I went to see my aunt, and immediately on my entering the room she said, 'O, Brother Newel, if you will lay your hands upon me, I shall be well and able to go on the journey with you.' I stepped up to the bed, and, in the name of the Lord Jesus Christ, rebuked the pain with which she was suffering, and commanded her to be made whole; and it was done; for the next morning she arose, dressed herself, and pursued the journey with us.

"We arrived at Buffalo without any further trouble, where we were to take passage on board a sloop for Fairport, Ohio. But the wind blew from the lake and filled the harbor with ice, so that we were detained nearly two weeks. When we set sail on the lake, the winds continued boisterous, and the vessel was tossed about in such a manner that nearly all the company were sea-sick, which made it rather a disagreeable voyage. We arrived safely, however, at our destination" (*Classic Experiences*, pp. 68–69).

LUCY MACK SMITH'S FAITH AND DETERMINATION

The same revelation that directed Hyrum Smith and Joseph Smith, Sr., to travel with the Colesville Saints also directed Lucy Smith and two of her sons to wait until spring, when they should go to Ohio with the Saints from the Waterloo-Fayette area.

Lucy Mack Smith recorded:

"When the brethren considered the spring sufficiently open for traveling on the water, we all began to prepare for our removal to Kirtland [February or March 1831]. We hired a boat of a certain Methodist preacher, and appointed a time to meet at our house, for the purpose of setting off together; and when we were thus collected, we numbered eighty souls. The people of the surrounding country came and bade us farewell, invoking the blessing of heaven upon our heads. . . .

"I then called the brethren and sisters together, and reminded them that we were traveling by commandment of the Lord, as much as Father Lehi was, when he left Jerusalem; and, if faithful, we had the same reasons to expect the blessings of God. I then desired them to be solemn, and to lift their hearts to God continually in prayer,

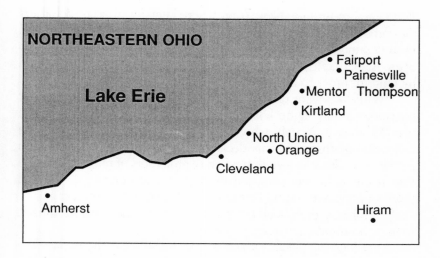

NORTHEASTERN OHIO

Lake Erie

• Fairport
• Painesville
•Mentor Thompson
• Kirtland
•North Union
• Orange
Cleveland
• Amherst
Hiram

that we might be prospered. We then seated ourselves and sang a hymn. The captain was so delighted with the music, that he called to the mate, saying, 'Do, come here, and steer the boat; for I must hear that singing.' He afterwards expressed his pleasure and surprise at seeing such an appearance of devotion among us, stating that his wife had refused to accompany him, on account of her prejudice against us, which he very much regretted.

"At the approach of sunset, we seated ourselves, and sang another hymn. The music sounded beautifully upon the water, and had a salutary effect upon every heart, filling our souls with love and gratitude to God, for his manifold goodness towards us.

"The services of the evening being ended, I inquired of the brethren concerning the amount of provisions which they had on hand for the journey; and, to my surprise, I ascertained that we had on board, besides twenty grown persons, thirty children, who were almost destitute of food. This was unaccountable to me at first, but I afterwards learned that they had converted their substance into clothing, expecting that those who were in better circumstances would support them, as well as defray their traveling expense; those, however, from whom they expected the most assistance, disappointed them, consequently, the burden was thrown entirely upon my shoulders. From this time forward, I furnished the whole fifty persons with food from day to day" (*History*, pp. 195–97).

The first part of their journey was made in a flatboat along the

Erie Canal to Buffalo, New York, where Lucy Smith and the others "found the brethren from Colesville, who informed us that they had been detained one week at this place, waiting for the navigation to open. Also, that Mr. Smith and Hyrum had gone through to Kirtland by land, in order to be there by the first of April. . . .

"While we were talking with the Colesville brethren, another boat landed, having on board about thirty brethren, among whom was Thomas B. Marsh, who immediately joined us, and, like the Colesville brethren, he was decidedly opposed to our attending to prayer, or making known that we were professors of religion. He said that if our company persisted in singing and praying, as we had hitherto done, we should be mobbed before the next morning.

" 'Mob it is, then,' said I, 'we shall attend to prayer before sunset, mob or no mob' " (History, p. 199).

After locating places for the people to stay near the harbor, the next morning Lucy Smith returned to the boat on the shore of Lake Erie. "On arriving there, Captain Blake requested the passengers to remain on board, as he wished, from that time, to be ready to start at a moment's warning; at the same time he sent out a man to measure the depth of the ice, who, when he returned, reported that it was piled up to the height of twenty feet, and that it was his opinion that we would remain in the harbor at least two weeks longer. . . .

"I went to that part of the boat where the principal portion of our company was. There I found several of the brethren and sisters engaged in a warm debate, others murmuring and grumbling, and a number of young ladies were flirting, giggling, and laughing with gentlemen passengers, who were entire strangers to them, whilst hundreds of people on shore and on other boats were witnessing this scene of clamor and vanity among our brethren with great interest. I stepped into their midst. 'Brethren and sisters,' said I, 'we call ourselves Saints, and profess to have come out from the world for the purpose of serving God at the expense of all earthly things; and will you, at the very onset, subject the cause of Christ to ridicule by your own unwise and improper conduct? You profess to put your trust in God, then how can you feel to murmur and complain as you do! You are even more unreasonable than the children of Israel were; for here are my sisters pining for their rocking chairs, and brethren from whom I expected firmness and energy, declare that they positively believe they shall starve to death before they get to the end of their journey. And why is it so? Have any of you lacked?

Have not I set food before you every day, and made you, who had not provided for yourselves, as welcome as my own children? Where is your faith? Where is your confidence in God? Can you not realize that all things were made by him, and that he rules over the works of his own hands? And suppose that all the Saints here should lift their hearts in prayer to God, that the way might be opened before us, how easy it would be for him to cause the ice to break away, so that in a moment we could be on our journey!' . . .

" . . . 'Now, brethren and sisters, if you will all of you raise your desires to heaven, that the ice may be broken up, and we be set at liberty, as sure as the Lord lives, it will be done.' At that instant a noise was heard, like bursting thunder. The captain cried, 'Every man to his post.' The ice parted, leaving barely a passage for the boat, and so narrow that as the boat passed through the buckets of the waterwheel were torn off with a crash, which, joined to the word of command from the captain, the hoarse answering of the sailors, the noise of the ice, and the cries and confusion of the spectators, presented a scene truly terrible. We had barely passed through the avenue when the ice closed together again, and the Colesville brethren were left in Buffalo, unable to follow us.

"As we were leaving the harbor, one of the bystanders exclaimed, 'There goes the "Mormon" company! That boat is sunk in the water nine inches deeper than ever it was before, and, mark it, she will sink—there is nothing surer.' In fact, they were so sure of it that they went straight to the office and had it published that we were sunk, so that when we arrived at Fairport we read in the papers the news of our own death.

"After our miraculous escape from the wharf at Buffalo, we called our company together and had a prayer meeting in which we offered up our thanks to God for his mercy, which he had manifested towards us in our deliverance" (*History*, pp. 202–5).

After arriving at Fairport Harbor, the group members became concerned about where they would stay temporarily and how they could transport themselves and their luggage to Kirtland. "My attention was attracted by a stranger, who sat a short distance from us on the shore of the lake. I inquired of him the distance to Kirtland. He, starting up, exclaimed, 'Is it possible that this is Mother Smith? I have sat here looking for you these three days.'

"Replying to his question in the affirmative, I asked him if it would be possible to procure teams to take our goods to Kirtland.

He told me to give myself no uneasiness about the matter, that Joseph was expected every hour, and in less than twenty-four hours there would be teams sufficient to take all our company to houses that were waiting to receive them. When he mentioned Joseph's name, I started, for I just began to realize that I was so soon to see both my husband and my sons. I turned from the stranger and met Samuel, who was coming towards me, closely followed by Joseph. I extended my right hand to Samuel and my left to Joseph. They wept for joy upon seeing me." In Painesville, "we stopped at the house of Brother Partridge. Here we found a fine supper prepared for the whole company" (*History*, pp. 206–7).

Emily, a young daughter of Edward Partridge, recalled how "the Saints began to gather to Kirtland from all parts of the country where the gospel had been preached; and as we lived about three miles from the landing, our house made a good stopping place for the Saints" ("Autobiography," p. 6).

10

CHALLENGES OF NEW CONVERTS

Doctrine and Covenants 41–51

The Prophet Joseph Smith recognized that the Saints were confronted with many problems relating to Church doctrine and administration. All the Saints were new converts, from diverse backgrounds, who brought with them a variety of beliefs and religious behavior. Between February and May 1831, Joseph received at Kirtland, Ohio, eleven revelations relating to proper Latter-day Saint beliefs and practices. Writings of contemporaries provide insights into the challenges that led to those instructions and help us understand the effect they had in the lives of the fledgling Saints.

COMMON STOCK REPLACED BY THE LORD'S LAW

Before their conversions, many of the Saints had been eager to restore primitive Christianity. To this end, they had sought specific guidelines in the New Testament. When they read that early Christians "had all things common" (Acts 4:32), they organized a system called "common stock," in which title to all property was held by the group rather than by individuals. The Prophet quickly discerned, however, that what they were doing was not in agreement with the Lord's will. "The disciples had all things common," John Whitmer recorded in his history, "and were going to destruction very fast as to temporal things; for they considered from reading the scripture that what belonged to a brother, belonged to any of the brethren. Therefore they would take each other's clothes and other property and use it without leave which brought on confusion and disappointment, for they did not understand the scripture" (*Early History*, p. 37). To remedy such problems, the Lord's first revelation in Ohio promised that he would reveal his "law" and called Edward Partridge to administer it as the Church's first bishop (D&C 41). Just a few days later, Joseph dictated a portion of what is today Doctrine and Covenants 42, which contains the moral code of the Church and basic elements of the law of consecration and stewardship. As a result, the Prophet recorded, "the plan of 'common stock,' which had existed in what was called 'the family,' whose members generally had embraced the everlasting Gospel, was readily abandoned for the more perfect law of the Lord; and the false spirits were easily discerned and rejected by the light of revelation" (History of the Church, 1:146–47).

WHO MAY RECEIVE REVELATION FOR THE CHURCH

Soon after the Lord's law was given through his authorized prophet, another person introduced confusion by "making great pretensions of revealing commandments, laws and other curious matters" (History of the Church, 1:154). Historian John Whitmer recorded:

"About these days there was a woman by the name of Hubble who professed to be a prophetess of the Lord and professed to have many revelations, and knew the Book of Mormon was true, and that she should become a teacher in the Church of Christ. She appeared to be very sanctimonious and deceived some who were not able to detect her in her hypocracy: others however had the spirit of discernment, and her follies and abominations were made manifest. The Lord gave Revelation that the saints might not be deceived [D&C 43]. . . .

"After this commandment was received, the saints came to understanding on this subject, and unity and harmony prevailed throughout the Church of God: and the Saints began to learn wisdom, and treasure up knowledge which they learned from the word of God, and by experience as they advanced in the way of eternal life" (Early History, pp. 42–44).

MISSION TO THE SHAKERS

One religious movement of the early nineteenth century was the United Believers in Christ's Second Coming, commonly nicknamed the "Shakers." Members of this group lived in several communities in the Northeastern United States. One of these communities, North Union, was only a few miles southwest of Kirtland. It was to this group of Shakers that the revelation in Doctrine and Covenants 49 directed Leman Copley, a convert from the Shakers, and other elders to go as missionaries. Soon afterwards, the missionaries attempted to share the gospel with these people but did not find success.

Ashbel Kitchell, leader of this Shaker community, recorded in his journal the coming of the Mormon missionaries: "We continued on friendly terms in the way of trade and other acts of good neighborship untill the spring of 1831 when we were visited on saturday evening by Sidney Rigdon and Leman Copley, the latter of whom had been among us; but not likeing the cross [the Shaker practice of celibacy] any to well, had taken up with Mormonism as the easier plan and had been appointed by them as one of the missionaries to convert us.

"They tarried all night, and in the course of the evening, the doctrines of the cross and the Mormon faith were both investigated; and we found that the life of . . . selfdenial corresponded better with the life of Christ, than Mormonism. . . . Thus the matter stood and we retired to rest, not knowing that they had then in possession what they called a revelation or message from Jesus Christ to us, which they intended to deliver to day (sabbath.) and which they supposed would bring us to terms.

"Sabbath morning, matters moved on pleasantly in sociable chat with the Brethren, untill I felt to give them all some council, which was for neither to force their doctrine on the other at this time; but let the time be spent in feeling of the spirit, as it was Rigdon's first visit, for it might be possible that he would yet see that the foundation he was now on, was sandy. . . .

" . . . A little before meeting, another one came from the Mormon camp as an assistant, by the name of Parley Pratt. He called them out, and enquired how they had got along? and was informed by Rigdon and Leman, that I had bound them to silence, and nothing could be done. Parley told them to pay no attention to me, for they had come with the authority of the Lord Jesus Christ, and the people must hear it, &c.

"They came into meeting and sat quietly untill the meeting was through, and the people dismissed; when Sidney Rigdon arose and stated that he had a message from the Lord Jesus Christ to this people; could he have the privilege of delivering it? He was answered, he could. He then said it was in writing; could he read it? He was told he might. He then read the following Message [The text of D&C 49, is here quoted with only a few minor wording changes from the way it appears in the Book of Comandments, chapter 52.].

"At the close of the reading, he asked if they could be permitted to go forth in the exercise of their gift and office. — I told him that the piece he had read, bore on its face, the image of its author; that the Christ that dictated that, I was well acquainted with, and had been, from a boy; that I had been much troubled to get rid of his influence, and I wished to have nothing more to do with him; and as for any gift he had authorized them to exercise among us, I would release them & their Christ from any further burden about us, and take all the responsibility on myself.

"Sidney made answer—This you . . . cannot do; I wish to hear the people speak. I told him if he desired it, they could speak for themselves, and steped back and told them to let the man know how they felt; which they did in something like these words; that they were fully satisfied with what they had, and wished to have nothing to do with either them or their Christ. On hearing this Rigdon professed to be satisfied, and put his paper by; but Parley Pratt arose and commenced shakeing his coattail; he said he shook the dust from his garments as a testimony against us, that we had rejected the word of the Lord Jesus.

"Before the words were out of his mouth, I was to him, and said;—You filthy Beast, dare you presume to come in here, and try to imitate a man of God by shaking your filthy tail; confess your sins and purge your soul from your lusts, and your other abominations before you ever presume to do the like again, &c. While I was ministering this reproof, he settled trembling into his seat, and covered his face; and I then turned to Leman who had been crying while the message was reading, and said to him, you hypocrite, you knew better;—you knew where the living work of God was. . . .

" . . . Leman tarried all night and started for home in the morning.

"He had a large farm, and about 100 Mormons were living with him, on it. When he got home, he found the Mormons had rejected him, & could not own him for one of them, because he had deceived them with the idea of converting us. He felt very bad;—was not able to rest;—came back to us and begged for union.

"After some consultation we concluded to give him union, and help him through; and to accomplish this, I went home with him, and held a meeting in the dooryard, among the Mormons; but few of them attended. They appeared to be struck with terror and fear lest some of them might get converted" (*BYU Studies*, Fall 1979, pp. 96–98).

DISCERNING SPIRITUAL MANIFESTATIONS

Doctrine and Covenants 46 and 50 deal specifically with gifts of the Spirit and how to detect false spiritual manifestations. Levi Hancock described the strange exercises of some converts in 1831: "Those elders ran into all manner of doings, receiving revelations and seeing angels. Falling down frothing at the mouth. . . . I have seen [one of them] jump up from the floor, strike his head against the joist in the Baldwins new house and swing some minutes, then fall like he was dead. After an hour or two he would come to. He would prophesy and tell what he had seen" ("Autobiography," p. 27).

Many years later, Elder George A. Smith recalled these problems in Kirtland. He declared that after the missionaries to the Lamanites left for Missouri and "Sidney Rigdon took a journey to the east, as did Edward Partridge for the purpose of visiting the Prophet" that "these strange spirits . . . began to manifest themselves in the churches and Branches which had been built up.

"There was at this time in Kirtland, a society that had undertaken to have a community of property; it has sometimes been denominated the Morley family, as there was a number of them located on a farm owned by Captain Isaac Morley. These persons had been baptized, but had not yet been instructed in relation to their duties. A false spirit entered into them, developing their singular, extravagant and wild ideas. They had a meeting at the farm, and among them was a negro known generally as Black Pete, who became a revelator. Others also manifested wonderful developments; they could see angels, and letters would come down from heaven, they said, and they would be put through wonderful unnatural distortions. Finally on one occasion, Black Pete got sight of one of those revelations . . . , he started after it, and ran off a steep wash bank twenty-five feet high, passed through a tree top into the Chagrin river beneath. He came out with a few scratches, and his ardor somewhat cooled.

"Joseph Smith came to Kirtland, and taught that people in relation to their error. He showed them that the Spirit of God did not bind men nor make them insane, and that the power of the adversary which had been manifested in many instances was visible even from that cause, for persons under its influence became helpless, and were bound hand and foot as in chains, being as immovable as a stick of timber. When Joseph came to instruct these Saints in relation to the true Spirit, and the manner of determining the one from the other, in a short time a number of those who had been influenced by those foul manifestations, apostatized" (*Journal of Discourses,* 11:3–4).

Parley P. Pratt also described behavior of the Saints that led him and others to seek counsel from the Prophet:

"As I went forth among the different branches, some very strange spiritual operations were manifested, which were disgusting, rather than edifying. Some persons would seem to swoon away, and make unseemly gestures, and be drawn or disfigured in their countenances. Others would fall into ecstacies, and be drawn into contortions, cramp, fits, etc. Others would seem to have visions and revelations, which were not edifying, and which were not congenial to the doctrine and spirit of the gospel. In short, a false and lying spirit seemed to be creeping into the Church.

"All these things were new and strange to me, and had originated in the Church during our absence, and previous to the arrival of President Joseph Smith from New York.

"Feeling our weakness and inexperience, and lest we should err in judgment concerning these spiritual phenomena, myself, John Murdock, and several other Elders, went to Joseph Smith, and asked him to inquire of the Lord concerning these spirits or manifestations.

"After we had joined in prayer in his translating room, he dictated in our presence the following revelation: [D&C 50]" (*Autobiography,* pp. 61–62). This revelation emphasized that the Lord's servants could discern the source of such manifestations by the Spirit and that spiritual gifts from God edify and help one to grow in light until reaching the "perfect day" (D&C 50:24).

11

A CALL TO ZION

Doctrine and Covenants 52–63

After a special conference at Kirtland early in June 1831, the Lord directed the elders to hold their next conference in the consecrated land of Missouri, where he would reveal the location of their inheritances (D&C 52:2, 5). The next four revelations, Doctrine and Covenants 53 through 56, given during that same month, directed other Saints to go to Missouri. Joseph Smith and those traveling with him arrived there in July. During the next few weeks in Missouri, the Prophet received six revelations (D&C 57–62), all related in one way or another to establishing Zion in that land.

THE COLESVILLE SAINTS MOVE TO MISSOURI

After Joseph Smith unfolded the law of consecration and stewardship (D&C 42:30–42), members of the Colesville branch who had settled in Thompson, Ohio, attempted to live this principle on land Leman Copley agreed to make available. Not long afterwards, however, he abruptly withdrew his offer, perhaps in the aftermath of his unsuccessful mission to the Shakers (see Chapter 10).

"At this time," John Whitmer recorded in his history, "the Church at Thompson Ohio was involved in difficulty, because of the rebellion of Lemon Copley who would not do as he had previously agreed, which thing confused the whole church" (*Early History*, p. 74). In the midst of this confusion, the Lord instructed Newel Knight to lead the Colesville Saints "unto the land of Missouri, unto the borders of the Lamanites" (D&C 54:8).

Complying with earlier revelations (D&C 37–38), Newel Knight had sold a choice farm in New York, which had lakes and streams, and moved to a wilderness in Thompson, Ohio. Traveling with the Colesville Saints, via the Ohio and Missouri Rivers, he reached the chosen land of Missouri and exclaimed, "our feelings can be better imagined than described, when we, found ourselves upon the

Western frontiers. The country itself presented a pleasant aspect with its rich forests bordering its beautiful streams, and its deep rolling prairies spreading far and wide, inviting the hand of industry to establish for itself homes upon its broad bosom. And this was the place, where the Lord had promised to reveal unto us where . . . the New Jerusalem" should be built. (*Classic Experiences*, p. 71).

DEDICATION OF THE CENTER PLACE

Newel Knight continued: "We had not long to wait, for during the month the Lord gave a revelation to Brother Joseph [soon after he arrived in Missouri], designating the spot [D&C 57:1–3].

"Being no longer at a loss to know where the exact spot for the building of the temple and the city of Zion was, we immediately prepared for our labors. On the 2nd day of August, Brother Joseph Smith, Jun., the prophet of God, assisted the Colesville branch to lay the first log as a foundation for Zion in Kaw township [now in Kansas City], twelve miles west of Independence. The log was carried by twelve men, in honor of the twelve tribes of Israel. . . . This was truly a season of joy and rejoicing to all the Saints, who took part in, or witnessed the proceedings" (*Classic Experiences*, p. 71).

Sidney Rigdon dedicated the land on this same occasion for the gathering of the Saints. He asked the converts if they would covenant to keep the commandments of God. After they responded positively, he said, "I now pronounce this land consecrated and dedicated to the Lord for a possession and inheritance for the Saints (in the name of Jesus Christ having authority from him.) And for all the faithful Servants of the Lord to the remotest ages of time" (Whitmer, *Early History*, p. 79).

The next day, August 3, a group of elders assembled on the rise where a temple was to be erected, and Joseph Smith dedicated the site. John Whitmer recorded: "Joseph Smith, Jr., laid a stone at the Northeast corner of the contemplated Temple in the name of the Lord Jesus of Nazareth. After all present had rendered thanks to the great ruler of the universe, Sidney Rigdon pronounced [that] Spot of ground wholly dedicated unto the Lord forever" (*Early History*, p. 80).

THE GATHERING TO ZION

Joseph Smith returned to Kirtland to find interest in Zion running high. In August 1831, the Lord declared that his Saints should "assemble themselves together unto the land of Zion" (D&C 63:24). The Lord had already directed Edward Partridge and his counselors in the bishopric to move with their families to Missouri (D&C 58:24–25). Consequently, the Partridge family were among the many Saints who migrated to Zion in the early 1830s. Reflections of Emily and Eliza, daughters of Edward and Lydia Partridge, reveal some challenges to the uprooted people. Born and raised in Painesville, Ohio, Eliza remembered that before her father was called to be bishop, he had a flourishing business, the family lived in a comfortable home, and she had "acquired a very good common education." When her father left his family to direct the business of the Church in Missouri in compliance with Doctrine and Covenants 58:24, he expected them to get along the best they could. "I was at that time, very sick," Eliza continued. Her father "had no expectation of seeing me again, but the Lord had called and he must obey. He showed his faith by his works and the Lord spared my life and the lives of the rest of his family for many years. He never went back to sell his place or settle his affairs, but left it for others to do which was done at a great sacrifice" (Lyman, "Autobiography," pp. 1–2).

Eliza's younger sister, Emily, also commented on the family's situation at the time of the move westward: "My mother felt that her trials had begun when my father was called to accompany the Prophet to Missouri [D&C 52:24]. . . . It was a new thing for her to be left alone in the hour of trouble, or to have any responsibility outside of her little family. . . .

"The next season mother with her family started for Missouri, in a company of Saints under the direction of W. W. Phelps and A. S. Gilbert. . . . We went down the Ohio River to Cincinnati in a keel boat. Then we took a steamboat and went up the Missouri River. . . . When we were within about one hundred miles of our destination we met the ice coming down the river so thick that the boat could not proceed and we were forced to land at a place called 'Arrow Rock.' On the banks of the river there was a log cabin occupied by Negroes. There were two rooms, with no windows. . . . These Negroes let mother and Sister Morley have one room. There was about fifteen in number in both families." There was a fireplace in the room in which they maintained a "good fire" that kept them from freezing. After living in the hut for a week or two, the families resumed their journey in a large Kentucky wagon. Emily remembered that the wagon in which she was riding was so tightly packed that she could hardly move when it stopped at Independence. Eventually, after some of the boxes had been unloaded and shifted, she succeeded in pulling herself out (Young, "Autobiography," pp. 7–9).

During the spring of 1832, Edward Partridge and his family moved into a house rented from Lilburn W. Boggs. Emily called it a small log room rather than a home. She remembered that because there was a shortage of homes in Independence during the winter of 1832–33, her father invited a widow with four children to live with his family. Consequently, twelve or thirteen people occupied one room. "Now don't think for a moment that we were crowded," Emily commented, "or that we children quarreled; perhaps we did, though I don't remember" (Young, "Autobiography," p. 10).

The family continued to live in that room until Bishop Partridge built a small log home near the temple lot, about one-half mile from the public square of Independence. It was constructed over a cellar and consisted of one room on the ground floor and one upstairs.

The Latter-day Saints assisted one another in building homes in the new land. Emily Partridge recorded that Church members periodically participated in "raisings." After logs had been gathered and prepared, "men in the neighborhood would turn out and lay them up. Raisings with the men were something like the old-fashioned quilting was with the women. . . . Some of the houses were built very neatly, the logs being hewn on the outside and inside, and the corners sawed off smooth, and for a log house they looked very respectable" (Young, "Autobiography," p. 11).

12

REVELATIONS AND EXPERIENCES IN HIRAM

Doctrine and Covenants 64–81

After returning to Kirtland from their first trip to Jackson County, Missouri, Joseph Smith and Sidney Rigdon moved their families to Hiram, Ohio, about thirty miles southeast of Kirtland. Joseph's family was invited to live in the farm home of John Johnson, and Sidney Rigdon moved into a small residence nearby.

THE JOHNSON FAMILY OF HIRAM, OHIO

John Johnson's home in Hiram, Ohio, was the headquarters of the Church for approximately six months, from mid September 1831 to late March 1832. During that time in Hiram, the Prophet Joseph Smith received fifteen revelations that are in the current edition of the Doctrine and Covenants (sections 1, 65, 67–69, 71, 73–74, 76–81, 133). Most of these revelations were received as he and his scribe, Sidney Rigdon, worked on the translation of the Bible. The revelations helped the Church members better understand the doctrines and administration of the restored Church.

Amos Hayden, a restorationist preacher and historian who was not a member of the Church, described an event that related to Joseph's being invited to move into the Johnson home: "Ezra Booth, of Mantua, a Methodist preacher of much more than ordinary culture, and with strong natural abilities, in company with his wife, Mr. and Mrs. Johnson, and some other citizens of this place [Hiram], visited Smith at his home in Kirtland, in 1831. Mrs. Johnson had been afflicted for some time with a lame arm, and was not at the time of the visit able to lift her hand to her head. The party visited Smith partly out of curiosity, and partly to see for themselves what there might be in the new doctrine. During the interview the conversation turned on the subject of supernatural gifts, such as were conferred in the days of the apostles. Some one said, 'Here is Mrs. Johnson with a lame arm; has God given any power to man now on the earth to cure her?'

"A few moments later, when the conversation had turned in another direction, Smith rose, and walking across the room, taking Mrs. Johnson by the hand, said in the most solemn and impressive manner: 'Woman, in the name of the Lord Jesus Christ I command thee to be whole,' and immediately left the room. The company were awe-stricken at the infinite presumption of the man, and the calm assurance with which he spoke. The sudden mental and moral shock—I know not how better to explain the well-attested fact— electrified the rheumatic arm—Mrs. Johnson at once lifted it up with ease, and on her return home the next day she was able to do her washing without difficulty or pain" (*History of the Church,* 215–16 n; see also *Journal of Discourses,* 11:4–5).

Philo Dibble described details of the setting of this miracle and events that occurred at the time of the healing of Elsa Johnson: "When Joseph came to Kirtland his fame spread far and wide. There was a woman living in the town of Hiram . . . who had a crooked arm, which she had not been able to use for a long period. She persuaded her husband, whose name was Johnson, to take her to Kirtland to get her arm healed.

"I saw them as they passed my house on their way. She went to Joseph and requested him to heal her. Joseph asked her if she believed the Lord was able to make him an instrument in healing her arm. She said she believed the Lord was able to heal her arm.

"Joseph put her off till the next morning, when he met her at Brother [Newel K.] Whitney's house. There were eight persons present, one a Methodist preacher, and one a doctor. Joseph took her by the hand, prayed in silence a moment, pronounced her arm whole, in the name of Jesus Christ, and turned and left the room.

"The preacher asked her if her arm was whole, and she straightened it out and replied: 'It is as good as the other' " (*Faith Promoting Classics,* p. 79).

A COMMAND TO FORGIVE

Just before moving to Hiram, the Prophet had received a revelation in which the Lord emphasized the Saints' responsibility to forgive (D&C 64:3–12). Joseph Smith had ample opportunity to put the Lord's counsel into practice before he left Hiram. On the night of 24 March 1832, Joseph and Emma stayed up late to take care of their sick twins. Joseph recounted that he had fallen asleep but "was soon after awakened by her [Emma] screaming murder, when I found myself going out of the door, in the hands of about a dozen men; some of whose hands were in my hair, and some had hold of my shirt, drawers and limbs. . . . I made a desperate struggle, as I was forced out, to extricate myself, but only cleared one leg, with which I made a pass at one man, and he fell on the door steps. I was immediately overpowered again; and they swore by G— —, they would kill me if I did not be still, which quieted me. As they passed around the house with me, the fellow that I kicked came to me and thrust his hand, all covered with blood, into my face and with an exulting hoarse laugh, muttered: 'Ge, gee, G—d— ye, I'l fix ye.'

"They then seized me by the throat and held on till I lost my breath. After I came to, as they passed along with me, about thirty rods from the house, I saw Elder Rigdon stretched out on the ground, whither they had dragged him by his heels. I supposed he was dead. I began to plead with them, saying, 'You will have mercy and spare my life, I hope.' To which they replied, 'G—d— ye, call on yer God for help, we'll show ye no mercy;' and the people began to show themselves in every direction; one coming from the orchard had a plank; and I expected they would kill me, and carry me off on the plank. They then turned to the right, and went on about thirty rods further; about sixty rods from the house, and thirty from where I saw Elder Rigdon, into the meadow, where they stopped, and one said, 'Simonds, Simonds,' (meaning, I supposed, Simonds Ryder [who had apostatized when the Prophet had misspelled his name in D&C 52:37],) 'pull up his drawers, pull up his drawers, he will take cold.' Another replied: 'Ain't ye going to kill 'im? ain't ye going to kill 'im?' when a group of mobbers collected a little way off, and said: 'Simonds, Simonds, come here;' and 'Simonds' charged those who had hold of me to keep me from touching the ground (as they had done all the time), lest I should get a spring upon them. They held a council, and as I could occasionally overhear a word, I supposed it was to know whether or not it was best to kill me. They returned after a while, when I learned that they had concluded not to kill me, but to beat and scratch me well, tear off my shirt and drawers, and leave me naked. One cried, 'Simonds, Simonds, where's the tar bucket?' 'I don't know,' answered one, 'where 'tis, Eli's left it.' They ran back and fetched the bucket of tar, when one exclaimed, with an oath, 'Let us tar up his mouth,' and they tried to force the tar-paddle into my mouth; I twisted my head around, so that they could not; and they cried out, 'G—d— ye, hold up yer head and let us giv ye some tar.' They then tried to force a vial into my mouth, and broke it in my teeth. All my clothes were torn off me except my shirt collar; and one man fell on me and scratched my body with his nails like a mad cat, and then muttered out: 'G—d— ye, that's the way the Holy Ghost falls on folks!'

"They then left me, and I attempted to rise, but fell again; I pulled the tar away from my lips, so that I could breathe more freely, and after a while I began to recover, and raised myself up, whereupon I saw two lights. I made my way towards one of them, and found it was Father Johnson's. When I came to the door I was naked, and the tar made me look as if I were covered with blood, and when my wife saw me she thought I was all crushed to pieces, and fainted. During the affray abroad, the sisters of the neighborhood had collected at my room. I called for a blanket, they threw me one and shut the door; I wrapped it around me and went in. . . .

"My friends spent the night in scraping and removing the tar, and washing and cleansing my body; so that by morning I was ready to be clothed again. This being the Sabbath morning, the people assembled for meeting at the usual hour of worship, and among them came also the mobbers; viz.: Simonds Ryder, a Campbellite preacher and leader of the mob; one McClentic, who had his hands in my hair; one Streeter, son of a Campbellite minister; and Felatiah Allen, Esq., who gave the mob a barrel of whiskey to raise their spirits. Besides these named, there were many others in the mob. With my flesh all scarified and defaced, I preached to the congregation as usual, and in the afternoon of the same day baptized three individuals.

"The next morning I went to see Elder Rigdon, and found him crazy, and his head highly inflamed, for they had dragged him by his heels, and those, too, so high from the ground that he could not raise his head from the rough, frozen surface, which lacerated it exceedingly . . . and he continued delirious some days. . . .

"During the mobbing one of the twins contracted a severe cold, continued to grow worse until Friday, and then died" [*History of the Church*, 1:261–65].

"THE VISION" OF THE DEGREES OF GLORY

The Prophet and Sidney Rigdon pondered many questions about the gospel while they were "translating" the Bible. For example, they wondered how scriptural references to "many mansions" could be harmonized with the teachings of most Christian churches that there is but one heaven and one hell. While the Prophet was living in the Johnson home, some of the most distinctive truths of the Restoration were unfolded during a vision of the degrees of glory (D&C 76).

Philo Dibble, who happened to enter the room while the vision was being received, stated that when "Joseph and Sidney were in the spirit and saw the heavens open, there were other men in the room, perhaps twelve, among whom I was one during a part of the time — probably two-thirds of the time, — I saw the glory and felt the power, but did not see the vision.

"The events and conversation, while they were seeing what is written (and many things were seen and related that are not written), I will relate as minutely as is necessary.

"Joseph would, at intervals, say: 'What do I see?' as one might say while looking out the window and beholding what all in the room could not see. Then he would relate what he had seen or what he was looking at. Then Sidney replied, 'I see the same.' Presently Sidney would say 'what do I see?' and would repeat what he had seen or was seeing, and Joseph would reply, 'I see the same.'

"This manner of conversation was repeated at short intervals to the end of the vision, and during the whole time not a word was spoken by any other person. Not a sound nor motion made by anyone but Joseph and Sidney, and it seemed to me that they never moved a joint or limb during the time I was there, which I think was over an hour, and to the end of the vision.

"Joseph sat firmly and calmly all the time in the midst of a magnificent glory, but Sidney sat limp and pale, apparently as limber as a rag, observing which, Joseph remarked, smilingly, 'Sidney is not used to it as I am' " (*Juvenile Instructor*, 15 May 1892, pp. 303–4).

Whenever the Prophet restored additional doctrines, some members became disaffected and left the Church. Brigham Young recalled in August 1852 his own mixed reaction to some of the ideas revealed in Doctrine and Covenants 76: "Many things which were revealed through Joseph came in contact with our own prejudices: we did not know how to understand them. . . . After all, my traditions were such, that when the Vision [D&C 76] came first to me, it was directly contrary and opposed to my former education. I said, Wait a little. I did not reject it; but I could not understand it. I then could feel what incorrect tradition had done for me. Suppose all that I have ever heard from my priest and parents—the way they taught me to read the Bible—had been true, my understanding would be diametrically opposed to the doctrine revealed in the Vision. I used to think and pray, to read and think, until I knew and fully understood it for myself, by the visions of the Holy Spirit" (*Journal of Discourses*, 6:280–81).

Persecution in Hiram continued to increase. Finally, in the spring of 1832, Joseph Smith and Sidney Rigdon were forced to leave Hiram and return to Kirtland, which again became the headquarters of the Church and the residence of the Prophet until 1838.

13

A CALL TO THE MINISTRY

Doctrine and Covenants 82–84

Having endured the oppression in Hiram and learning of mob threats in Kirtland, in April 1832 Joseph Smith traveled to Missouri, from where he directed the affairs of the Church. Then, after receiving two revelations in Jackson County (D&C 82–83), he returned to Ohio. The Prophet and Sidney Rigdon moved to Kirtland with their families, and, believing that he would be protected by the Saints, Joseph settled there. From the summer of 1832 until January 1838, Kirtland was the major center of the Church and the base from which many missionaries were sent forth.

Church members remodeled the attic of Newel K. Whitney's store to make an apartment for the Prophet and his family. The store continued to be the private business of Newel K. Whitney and served as the local post office. When Newel Whitney was called to serve as the bishop of the Church in the East, his store became a bishop's storehouse. For several years, the building was also the headquarters of the Church and the site where Joseph Smith received many revelations and visions. In fact, between September 1832 and December 1833, sixteen revelations (84–98, 101) were received in Kirtland.

Even though Doctrine and Covenants 84 is often thought of as a "revelation on priesthood," another major theme is missionary work. Many were called by revelation to labor in the ministry. Section 84 was recorded in September 1832 when a group of elders returned from missions in the Eastern states and reported their activities. In this revelation, the Lord reminded the missionaries that their duty was to convert and baptize and that "signs would follow them that believe" (D&C 84:64–74). Reports by early missionaries described their success and attested that God's power was manifest among these elders and the members of the Church.

MISSIONARIES AND MIRACLES

One of the many elders who labored in 1832 and kept a journal of his experiences was Jared Carter: "We arrived in Kirtland on the evening of the 19th of October, 1832, where I met with some of my brethren and heard them read revelations which caused my heart to rejoice. . . . Now while I make this record," he wrote "I remember the goodness of the Lord to me in the mission that I have lately been to in the east. . . . All that have been baptized while I have been in the regions where I have been in this mission is 98 and many others have been convinced of the work, that sooner or later, I think, will obey the work. I have been directed by the Spirit to bless in the name of Christ in many places or houses and I have found even by what "I have seen and heard that the consequences of blessing has been like leavening among measures of meal and now I can say, 'Bless the Lord, O my soul, for the marvelous works that He has done since I have come to this work.'

"I have seen many marvelous manifestations of the power of God in more than eighty instances, by the instrumentality of myself and other elders in this Church of Christ. Many of which miracles I have recorded in my journals."

One such manifestation "took place in the town of Willsbury, New York State, Essex County. This was a woman that had been lame for some time. She was deprived of the use of her legs so that she could not walk. I conversed with her to convince her of the truth of the Book of Mormon and she became convinced but she could not walk therefore she could not obey the gospel. I asked her if she would obey if God would give her power to walk. She promised that she would. I then took her by the hand and commanded her, in the name of Jesus Christ, to walk and the God of heaven gave her power to walk. This woman was called by the name of French and I was informed by the people that she was not able to walk, only by the help of crutches and this she was enabled to do only by the following manner: by the help of two crutches, putting them one under each arm then bearing the weight of her body thereon to put both of her feet a short space forward and in this way she could move around some but now, notwithstanding, she could walk considerably well and she used her crutches no more as I ever heard of" ("Autobiography," pp. 20–21).

Jared Carter also included in his journal an account of the healing of John Tanner: "On Sunday we held a meeting at Brother Tanner's and found the pleasure of the Lord was powerfully manifested. After the meeting we baptized. We found while here the Lord had mercy upon a lame man by the name of Tanner, who was so lame that he could not bear his weight on one of his feet. He had been lame for months but we found that he was a believer in the Book of Mormon. I asked him to endeavor to walk in the name of Christ and he agreed to undertake. I then took him by the hand and commanded him in the name of Christ to walk and by the power of Christ he was enabled to walk. Brother Simeon was not that moment present but I found after this, at the very time he was healed, Brother Simeon had an exercise of faith for him in secret prayer to God" ("Autobiography," p. 19).

CONVERTS SHARE THE GOSPEL

One of the converts taught by Jared Carter was Zera Pulsipher, who also described the faith-promoting incidents that led to and followed his conversion:

"In the summer of 1831 I heard a minister [speak of] an ancient record or Golden Bible in Manchester near Palmyra which remark struck me like a shock of electricity. At the same time [I] thought it might be something that would give light to my mind upon principles that I had been thinking of for years and many times I had remarked that if the pure church with its gifts and graces was on the earth, if so I had not found it. But I should be happy enough to find it in my day.

"I embraced it accordingly in the fall of 1831 there was a Book of Mormon brought in to town I succeeded in getting it. I directly read it through twice gave it a thorough investigation and believed it was true and the winter following Jerod Carter came that was from a mission to Vermont or Lake George. As soon as he came into town I, with two Methodist Preachers went to see him. After a reasonable introduction I questioned him upon the principles of the ancient gospel with all its gifts belonging to it. I asked him if he believed it, he answered in the affirmative. I asked him if he had ever laid hands on the sick and they had recovered. Yes, he said, he had in many instances.

"He preached the following evening to a crowded congregation, held up the Book of Mormon and declared it to be a revelation from God. I could not gain-say anything he had said, he sat down and gave liberty for remarks, the congregation seemed to be in amaze not knowing what to think of what they had heard. I arose and said to the congregation that we had been hearing strange things and if true they were of the utmost importance to us. If not true it was one of the greatest impositions and as the preacher had said that he had got his knowledge from heaven and was nothing but a man and I the same, that I had just as good a right to obtain that blessing as he, therefore I was determined to have that knowledge for myself which I considered it my privilege, from that time I made it a matter of fervent prayer.

"I think about the seventh day as I was thrashing in my barn with doors shut, all at once there seemed to be a ray of light from heaven which caused me to stop work for a short time, but soon began it again. Then in a few minutes another light came over my head which caused me to look up. I thought I saw the angels with the Book of Mormon in their hands in the attitude of showing it to me and saying 'this is the great revelation of the last days in which all things spoken of by the prophets must be fulfilled.' The vision was so open and plain that I began to rejoice exceedingly so that I walked the length of my barn crying 'Glory Hal-la-lu-ya to the God and the Lamb forever.'

"For some time it seemed a little difficult to keep my mind in a proper state of reasonable order, I was so filled with the joys of heaven. But when my mind became calm I called the church together [he was their minister] and informed them of what I had seen. I told them of my determination to join the Church of Latter Day Saints, which I did and a large body of my church went with me. I was ordained to the office of an elder and went to preaching with considerable success at home and abroad. I had the privilege of baptizing Wilford Woodruff on the 31st of December, 1833, at Richland, New York" ("Autobiography," pp. 5–7).

During his first mission in 1833, Zera Pulsipher and his companion, Elijah Cheney, introduced the gospel to Wilford Woodruff, who had been influenced by his friend Robert Mason to seek a restored church led by apostles and prophets. As explained in Wilford Woodruff's writings: "Father Mason did not claim that he had any authority to officiate in the ordinances of the gospel, nor did he believe that such authority existed on the earth. He did believe, however, that it was the privilege of any man who had faith in God to fast and pray for the healing of the sick by the laying on of hands. He believed it his right and the right of every honest-hearted man or woman to receive light and knowledge, visions, and revelations by the prayer of faith. He told me that the day was near when the Lord would establish His Church and Kingdom upon the earth with all its ancient gifts and blessings. He said that such a work would commence upon the earth before he died, but that he would not live to partake of its blessings. He said that I should live to do so, and that I should become a conspicuous actor in that kingdom" (Cowley, *Wilford Woodruff*, p. 16).

One day, when Wilford returned from working in his fields, his sister-in-law told him of a meeting being conducted by Mormon missionaries. "I immediately turned out my horses and started for the schoolhouse without waiting for supper. On my way I prayed most sincerely that the Lord would give me His spirit, and that if these men were the servants of God I might know it, and that my heart might be prepared to receive the divine message they had to deliver.

"When I reached the place of meeting, I found the house already packed. My brother Azmon was there before I arrived. He was equally eager to hear what these men had to say. I crowded my way through the assembly and seated myself upon one of the writing desks where I could see and hear everything that took place.

"Elder Pulsipher opened with prayer. He knelt down and asked the Lord in the name of Jesus Christ for what he wanted. His manner of prayer and the influence which went with it impressed me greatly. The spirit of the Lord rested upon me and bore witness that he was a servant of God. After singing, he preached to the people for an hour and a half. The spirit of God rested mightily upon him and he bore a strong testimony of the divine authenticity of the Book of Mormon and of the mission of the Prophet Joseph Smith. I believed all that he said. The spirit bore witness of its truth. Elder Cheney then arose and added his testimony to the truth of the words of Elder Pulsipher." After the meeting, Wilford began reading the Book of Mormon. "As I did so," he wrote, "the spirit bore witness that the record which it contained was true. I opened my eyes to see, my ears to hear, and my heart to understand. I also opened my doors to entertain the servants of God" (Cowley, *Wilford Woodruff*, pp. 33–34).

On December 31, the last day of the year 1833, Wilford and his brother Azmon requested baptism at the hands of the elders. They were baptized about eleven o'clock in the morning in the presence of a large number of people. The elders also baptized two young women who had been healed the day before. Wilford Woodruff recorded this event in his journal: "The snow was about three feet deep, the day was cold, and the water was mixed with ice and snow, yet I did not feel the cold" (Cowley, *Wilford Woodruff*, p. 35).

On 25 January 1834, Elder Pulsipher organized the Saints in Richland into a branch of the Church. He ordained Wilford Woodruff to the office of a teacher and gave him a written license that embodied the certificate of his baptism and his ordination. Wilford Woodruff prayed earnestly that he would receive a missionary call. Finally, in November 1834, Elias Higbee approached him and said, "Brother Wilford, the spirit of the Lord tells me that you should be ordained to go and preach the gospel." A few days later he was ordained a priest and was called to serve in Arkansas and Tennessee (Cowley, *Wilford Woodruff*, pp. 46–47). The convert Wilford Woodruff became one of the most successful missionaries in the history of the Church.

14

"STAND YE IN HOLY PLACES"
Doctrine and Covenants 86–88

In December 1832 while living in an apartment above Newel K. Whitney's store, the Prophet received three revelations (D&C 86–88) pertaining to conditions preceding the second coming of Christ. Section 87 is the often quoted "prophecy on war." Section 88 directs the elders to form the School of the Prophets so that they might be prepared to bear testimony to the world before the destructions and tribulations that will precede the Second Coming.

PROPHECY ON WAR

On Christmas Day, Joseph Smith received a revelation prophesying "wars that will shortly come to pass beginning at the rebellion of South Carolina" (D&C 87:1). He was well aware of rebellion already taking place in South Carolina: "the United States, amid all her pomp and greatness, was threatened with immediate dissolution. The people of South Carolina, in convention assembled (in November), passed ordinances, declaring their state a free and independent nation; and appointed Thursday, the 31st day of January, 1833, as a day of humiliation and prayer, to implore Almighty God to vouchsafe His blessings, and restore liberty and happiness within their borders. President [Andrew] Jackson issued his proclamation against this rebellion, called out a force sufficient to quell it, and implored the blessings of God to assist the nation to extricate itself from the horrors of the approaching and solemn crisis" (*History of the Church*, 1:301).

This "rebellion of South Carolina" did not directly lead to the American Civil War, however. South Carolina had objected to a high tariff proposed by the federal government, but no other states came to her side. In 1833, Congress enacted a compromise tariff bill, and the conflict subsided. More than a decade after receiving the revelation recorded in Doctrine and Covenants 87, the Prophet learned by inspiration that the Civil War would grow out of yet another crisis in South Carolina and over an entirely different issue (D&C 130:12–13).

The prophecy on war and manuscripts of the Joseph Smith Translation of the Bible were in the possession of James Mulholland, Joseph Smith's private secretary, at the time of the Saints' expulsion from Missouri during the winter of 1838–39. While living at Far West, James Mulholland gave these records to one of his relatives, Ann Scott, for safekeeping. She wrote that the mob "frequently searched my father's house, and were very insulting in their deportment. They also searched other houses of the Saints, including that of President Joseph Smith, who at the time was confined in Liberty Jail. Joseph's confinement in prison, coupled with the ruthless invasions of the mob, caused his scribe, Elder James Mulholland, to seek a place of safety for important church papers in his possession. . . . Brother Mulholland requested me to take charge of these papers, as he thought they would be more secure with me, because I was a woman, and the mob would not be likely to search my person. Immediately on taking possession of the papers, I made two cotton bags of sufficient size to contain them, sewing a band around the top ends of sufficient length to button around my waist; and I carried those papers on my person in the day-time, when the mob was round, and slept with them under my pillow at night. I cannot remember now the exact length of time I had those papers in my possession; but I gave them to sister Emma Smith, the prophet's wife, on the evening of her departure for Commerce" ("Spiritual Reminiscences," in *Autumn Leaves* (1891), 4:18).

THE SCHOOL OF THE PROPHETS

On 27 December 1832, two days after Joseph Smith recorded the prophecy on war, a conference of high priests assembled in the translating room in the apartment above Newel K. Whitney's store. After the invocation, Joseph said, "To receive revelation and the blessings of heaven it was necessary to have our minds on God and exercise faith and become of one heart and of one mind" (Kirtland Council Minute Book, pp. 3–4). Therefore, he recommended, all present should pray separately and vocally to the Lord to receive his will regarding those present and the building of Zion. All knelt in prayer, after which all arose and spoke, describing their feelings and commitment to keep the commandments of the Lord. During that meeting, the Prophet received the revelation that is now Doctrine and Covenants 88.

In this revelation was a commandment to organize a School of the Prophets (D&C 88:70–80, 117–41) and build a house of the Lord (see Chapter 16). The School was organized during a period of spiritual manifestations in Kirtland. As explained in Joseph Smith's history: "This winter [1832–33] was spent in translating the Scriptures; in the School of the Prophets; and sitting in conferences. I had many glorious seasons of refreshing. The gifts which follow them that believe and obey the Gospel, as tokens that the Lord is ever the same in His dealings with the humble lovers and followers of truth, began to be poured out among us, as in ancient days. . . . On the 22nd day of January, I spoke to the conference in another tongue, and was followed in the same gift by Brother Zebedee Coltrin, and he by Brother William Smith, after which the Lord poured out His Spirit in a miraculous manner, until all the Elders spake in tongues, and several members, both male and female, exercised the same gift. Great and glorious were the divine manifestations of the Holy Spirit. Praises were sung to God and the Lamb; speaking and praying, all in tongues, occupied the conference until a late hour at night, so rejoiced were we at the return of these long absent blessings.

"On the 23rd of January, we [members of the School of the Prophets] again assembled in conference; when, after much speaking, singing, praying, and praising God, all in tongues, we proceeded to the washing of feet (according to the practice recorded in the 13th chapter of John's Gospel), as commanded of the Lord [D&C 88:74–75]. Each Elder washed his own feet first, after which I girded myself with a towel and washed the feet of all of them, wiping them with the towel with which I was girded. . . .

"I then said to the Elders, As I have done so do ye; wash ye, therefore, one another's feet; and by the power of the Holy Ghost I pronounced them all clean from the blood of this generation; but if any of them should sin wilfully after they were thus cleansed, and sealed up unto eternal life, they should be given over unto the buffetings of Satan until the day of redemption. Having continued all day in fasting, and prayer, and ordinances, we closed by partaking of the Lord's supper. I blessed the bread and wine in the name of the Lord, when we all ate and drank, and were filled; then we sang a hymn, and the meeting adjourned" (History of the Church, 1:322–24).

Zebedee Coltrin, who was present when the School of the Prophets was organized on 23 January 1833, stated that the salutation written in the Doctrine and Covenants (D&C 88:136–41) was carried out during the first meeting of the School of the Prophets and "at every meeting." "The washing of feet was attended to," he added, and "the sacrament was also administered at times when Joseph appointed, after the ancient order."

Zebedee Coltrin also recalled that "every time we were called together to attend to any business, we came together in the morning about sunrise, fasting and partook of the sacrament each time, and before going to school we washed ourselves and put on clean linen" (Minutes, Salt Lake School of Prophets, 3 Oct. 1883, p. 56).

A highlight of the School of the Prophets occurred on March 18. After Joseph promised members of the School that "the pure in heart should see a heavenly vision," a group of elders engaged "in secret prayer." Then "the promise was verified; for many present had the eyes of their understanding opened by the Spirit of God," Joseph testified, "so as to behold many things. I then blessed the bread and wine, and distributed a portion to each. Many of the brethren saw a heavenly vision of the Savior, and concourses of angels, and many other things, of which each one has a record of what he saw" (*History of the Church*, 1:334–35).

Zebedee Coltrin witnessed this vision. He recalled that while they were praying, they beheld two personages who were identified by the Prophet as the Father and the Son. He "experienced a sensation," he explained, like a "consuming fire of great brightness." The Prophet Joseph said this was the Father of our Lord Jesus Christ. The Father "was surrounded as with a flame of fire, which was so brilliant that I could not discover anything else but his person. I saw his hands, his legs, his feet, his eyes, nose, mouth, head and body in the shape and form of a perfect man. . . . This appearance was so grand and overwhelming that it seemed I should melt down in his presence, and the sensation was so powerful that it thrilled through my whole system and I felt it in the marrow of my bones." Zebedee Coltrin further stated that the Prophet told them, "Brethren, now you are prepared to be the apostles of Jesus Christ, for you have seen both the Father and the Son and know that they exist and that they are two separate personages" (Minutes, Salt Lake School of Prophets, 3 Oct. 1883, p. 56).

The first session of the School of the Prophets closed in April

1833. Apparently, when a new group gathered in the fall, the elders did not continue participating in the ordinance of the washing of the feet. This rite was reintroduced among bearers of the priesthood a few days after the dedication of the Kirtland Temple (*History of the Church*, 2:430).

15

THE LORD'S LAW OF HEALTH

Doctrine and Covenants 89

One of the best-known revelations in the Doctrine and Covenants is section 89, the Word of Wisdom. The proponents of temperance had created a climate in which these divinely revealed principles could be accepted more readily.

SETTING FOR THE REVELATION

In 1830, Sylvester Graham, a former Presbyterian minister who was serving as president of the Pennsylvania Temperance Society, delivered in Philadelphia a series of lectures on health. He said in essence that five poisons were afflicting the American public: liquor, tobacco, tea, coffee, and opium. He advanced a system of diet in which adults were to abstain from eating meat, gravy, spices, cheese, and eggs and to refrain from drinking milk. He further advocated that individuals should drink rain water and eat fresh fruits and vegetables and bread made from unsifted flour. Although his name has since been relegated to a few items on grocery store shelves, such as graham crackers and graham bread, Sylvester Graham became one of America's leading health advocates before the Civil War.

There is no evidence that Joseph Smith learned about the Graham system prior to unfolding the Word of Wisdom, but it is known that ideas popularized by Sylvester Graham were being discussed in various journals of health. Graham acknowledged that he was influenced by reading the writings of others. As a man, Joseph Smith did not have the education or the background necessary to select correct principles from the myriad of health ideas and fads that were being circulated by his generation; but, as a prophet, he recorded enduring principles of health that have been substantiated by twentieth-century research (Backman, *Heavens Resound*, p. 236).

The most detailed description of the immediate setting of the Word of Wisdom (Section 89) was given in a sermon by President Brigham Young in February 1868:

"When the school of the prophets was inaugurated, one of the first revelations given by the Lord to His servant Joseph was the Word of Wisdom. The members of that school were but a few at first, and the prophet commenced to teach them in doctrine to prepare them to go out into the world to preach the gospel unto all people, and gather the elect from the four quarters of the earth, as the prophets anciently have spoken. . . . I think I am as well acquainted with the circumstances which led to the giving of the Word of Wisdom as any man in the Church, although I was not present at the time to witness them. The first school of the prophets was held in a small room situated over the Prophet Joseph's kitchen, in a house which belonged to Bishop Whitney, and which was attached to his store, which store probably might be about fifteen feet square. In the rear of this building was a kitchen, probably ten by fourteen feet, containing rooms and pantries. Over this kitchen was situated the room in which the Prophet received revelations and in which he instructed his brethren. The brethren came to that place for hundreds of miles to attend school in a little room probably no larger than eleven by fourteen. When they assembled together in this room after breakfast, the first they did was to light their pipes, and, while smoking, talk about the great things of the kingdom, and spit all over the room, and as soon as the pipe was out of their mouths a large chew of tobacco would then be taken. Often when the Prophet entered the room to give the school instructions he would find himself in a cloud of tobacco smoke. This, and the complaints of his wife at having to clean so filthy a floor, made the Prophet think upon the matter, and he inquired of the Lord relating to the conduct of the Elders in using tobacco, and the revelation known as the Word of Wisdom was the result of his inquiry" (*Journal of Discourses*, 12:157–58).

ACCEPTANCE OF THE WORD OF WISDOM

Zebedee Coltrin remembered that after the Prophet came out of the translating room, he read the revelation on the Word of Wisdom to members of the School of the Prophets. "Twenty out of the twenty-one" present, he said, "used tobacco and they all immediately threw their tobacco and pipes into the fire" (Minutes, Salt Lake School of Prophets, 13 Oct. 1883, pp. 55–56).

Joel Johnson was present when the revelation was introduced to members of the Church, and he recalled some of the challenges and controversies that confronted members as they attempted to abide by this law of health:

"I was then [February 1833] thirty one years of age, and had used tobacco somewhat extravagantly for fifteen years. I always used some strong drink, and tea and coffee.

"I knew that God had spoken and condemned the use of these things, and, being determined to live by every word that proceeded from His mouth, I laid them all aside, and have not used them since.

"I well remember that, soon after the publication of the Word of Wisdom, the same excuse was made, by some of the people, for drinking tea and coffee that is now made—that hot drinks did not mean tea and coffee.

"On a Sabbath day, in the July following the giving of the revelation, when both Joseph and Hyrum Smith were in the stand, the Prophet said to the Saints:

" 'I understand that some of the people are excusing themselves in using tea and coffee, because the Lord only said "hot drinks" in the revelation of the Word of Wisdom.'

" 'The Lord was showing us what was good for man to eat and drink. Now, what do we drink when we take our meals?'

" 'Tea and coffee. Is it not?'

" 'Yes; tea and coffee.'

" 'Then, they are what the Lord meant when He said 'hot drinks.'

"Brother Hyrum Smith spoke to the same effect.

"It is said all wholesome herbs are ordained for the use of man. Physicians tell us that tea and coffee are not wholesome. And the Lord says they are not for the body or the belly.

"When children see that their parents slight the Word of Wisdom, they are apt to follow their example.

"I have recorded this testimony that all who read it may be without excuse. How pleasant it would be at last, if we could say to our Heavenly Father, 'I have obeyed all your counsels,' and hear these kind words in return: 'Well done! thou hast been faithful over a few things, be thou ruler over many' " (*Voice from the Mountains*, pp. 12–13).

Many members of the Church confirmed in their writings that the phrase "hot drinks" was interpreted as tea and coffee. Elizabeth Tanner recorded her response to the revelation: "When the Word of Wisdom was preached we discarded the use of tea, coffee, and spirituous liquors," for she and her husband, John Tanner, strove diligently to observe "all of the laws of the Church" ("Autobiography," p. 1).

Although various quorums of the Church voted that the Saints should totally abstain from using alcohol, tobacco, and hot drinks (tea and coffee), serious problems developed over a strict application of these policies. Because of the Saints' widespread use of these substances and their deep-seated attachment to them, by mid 1834 many emphasized that the preface said that this revelation was to be regarded as general advice, not as a commandment. Even so, zealous leaders and members pressed for compliance with the original meaning of the revelation, and, in early December 1836, a vote of the Saints in Kirtland unanimously banned "all liquors from the Church," even during sickness, except for wine for the sacrament and liquor for "external washing" ("Journal of Wilford Woodruff"; Backman and Cook, *Kirtland Elders' Quorum Record*, p. 32). The policy, however, continued to be a controversial issue, and many Saints believed that the use of stimulants during sickness, fatigue, and depression was not in violation of the Word of Wisdom. Subsequently, there are many casual references in Joseph Smith's history of Church members drinking wine.

Throughout the early history of the Church, many members struggled to discontinue smoking, chewing tobacco, and drinking tea, coffee, and alcoholic beverages. Mary Winters, whose mother married Parley P. Pratt after the death of Elder Pratt's wife, described her mother's plan to conquer her temptations: "In those early days, snuff-taking was quite fashionable. My father had given mother a very pretty snuff box, and though she had not practiced using snuff herself, she had the box filled and a nice vanilla bean in it to scent the snuff, and when old ladies came to see her, she would pass it around to them. It was also customary for people in trouble to smoke or take snuff to soothe their feelings and pass away the time (poor souls), and this course was urged upon mother. Smoking she could not think of, as it seemed too troublesome a habit, but she had become quite used to taking snuff before she heard the gospel sound. But now after hearing the Word of Wisdom taught, she must not partake of the forbidden snuff any longer. And in her patriarchal blessing too, Word of Wisdom was spelled with large letters, so now the sacrifice must surely begin. It was her habit, immediately after eating, to take a pinch of snuff, but now instead, she placed the snuff box on the chimney piece over the letters and above the crickets, and took the Book of Mormon and sat down to read until all desire for the snuff had passed — and thus she gained the victory, with the temptation in plain sight. And oh how thankful she was in after years for the knowledge of the evil, and for the strength to overcome it" ("Autobiography," p. 3).

16

BUILDING THE LORD'S HOUSE IN KIRTLAND

Doctrine and Covenants 94–95

On 27 December 1832, in the revelation known as the Olive Leaf, the Saints were commanded to establish in Kirtland a house of prayer, fasting, faith, learning, glory, and order (D&C 88:119). This command was fulfilled with construction of the Kirtland Temple. In May 1833, the Saints were directed to plan two additional structures: a building for the presidency, and another for printing (D&C 94).

When the Prophet recorded the commandment to build a temple in Kirtland, there were only about one hundred members, or about twenty families, in that community, most of the earlier Saints having moved on to Missouri. Latter-day Saints living there were relatively poor—certainly none could be considered wealthy—and no Church members in Kirtland had the architectural skills essential for constructing a large building. Yet, the writings of contemporaries testify that amid poverty and persecution, Latter-day Saints sacrificed and performed a modern miracle.

THE LORD REVEALS THE DESIGN OF THE KIRTLAND TEMPLE

On 1 June 1833, the Lord explained the functions of the two main auditoriums of the temple and promised to reveal how the building should be designed (D&C 95:14–17). Two days later, a council of high priests met to discuss how the building should be constructed. According to the Prophet's mother, Lucy Mack Smith, "In this council, Joseph requested that each of the brethren should give his views with regard to the house; and when they had all got through, he would give his opinion concerning the matter. They all complied with his request. Some were in favor of building a frame house, but others were of a mind to put up a log house. Joseph reminded them that they were not building a house for a man, but for God; 'and shall we, brethren,' said he, 'build a house for our God, of logs? No, I have a better plan than that. I have a plan of the house of the Lord, given by himself; and you will soon see by this, the difference between our calculations and his idea of things.'

"He then gave them a full pattern of the house of the Lord at Kirtland, with which the brethren were highly delighted. . . .

"After the close of the meeting, Joseph took the brethren with him, for the purpose of selecting a spot for the building to stand upon. The place which they made choice of was situated in the north-west corner of a field of wheat, which was sown by my sons the fall previous, on the farm upon which we were then living. In a few minutes the fence was removed, and the standing grain was levelled, in order to prepare a place for the building and Hyrum commenced digging a trench for the wall, he having declared that he would strike the first blow upon the house" (*History*, pp. 230–31.)

Other contemporaries testified that the plans of this building were revealed to the First Presidency through visions and revelations. Orson Pratt declared that the Prophet and others learned by revelation not only about the size of the house but about the "order of the pulpits" and "various courts and apartments." Joseph was "strictly commanded to build according to the pattern revealed from the heavens" (*Journal of Discourses*, 13:357).

Architect Truman O. Angell also attested to divine direction in designing the temple. He recorded a conversation between one of the workmen who built the temple and Fredrick G. Williams, a member of the First Presidency. One day when Frederick G. Williams was in the temple, "Carpenter Rolph said: 'Doctor [Williams], what do you think of the House?'

"He answered, 'It looks to me like the pattern precisely.' Then he related the following: 'Joseph received the word of the Lord for him to take his two counselors, [Frederick G.] Williams and [Sidney] Rigdon, and come before the Lord, and He would show them the plan or model of the house to be built. We went upon our knees, called on the Lord, and the building appeared within viewing distance: I being the first to discover it. Then all of us viewed it together. After we had taken a good look at the exterior, the building seemed to come right over us; and the make-up of this hall seemed to coincide with what I there saw to a minutia.'

"Joseph was accordingly enabled to dictate to the mechanics, and his counselors stood as witnesses" (*Improvement Era*, Oct. 1942, p. 630).

THE SAINTS UNITE TO BUILD THE LORD'S HOUSE

The Lord has revealed that his Saints must sacrifice to build houses to his name (D&C 97:12). Nearly all the Latter-day Saints united in building the Kirtland Temple for the Lord. Eliza R. Snow wrote:

"With very little capital except brain, bone and sinew, combined with unwavering trust in God, men, women, and even children, worked with their might; while the brethren labored in their departments, the sisters were actively engaged in boarding and clothing workmen not otherwise provided for — all living as abstemiously as possible so that every cent might be appropriated to the grand object, while their energies were stimulated by the prospect of participating in the blessing of a house built by the direction of the Most High and accepted by him" (Tullidge, *Women of Mormondom*, p. 82).

When Heber C. Kimball arrived in Kirtland, he noticed that the Prophet didn't just direct the construction; he worked alongside the others in building the temple. "Joseph said, 'Come, brethren, let us go into the stone-quarry and work for the Lord.' And the Prophet went himself, in his tow frock and tow breeches, and worked at quarrying stone like the rest of us. Then, every Saturday we brought out every team to draw stone to the Temple, and so we continued until that house was finished; and our wives were all the time knitting, spinning and sewing, and, in fact, I may say doing all kinds of work; they were just as busy as any of us, and I say that those women have borne the heat and burden of those early and trying days and God will bless them for evermore" (*Journal of Discourses*, 10:165).

Church membership increased from one hundred to nearly one thousand during the time the temple was being built, but the Saints' poverty persisted. Nearly all the converts gathered to Kirtland from other areas, many from New England and New York. Most had to leave belongings behind and to sacrifice financially to make the move. When they arrived, instead of buying land and homes or otherwise improving their own standard of living, many sacrificed a portion of their material means to support various Church programs, notably building the temple.

One immigrant to Kirtland, Jonathan Crosby, recalled an

incident that illustrates the poverty of the Saints in 1836: "Shortly after our arrival in Kirtland, brothers Brigham Young, Heber C. Kimball, and Parley P. Pratt, came to me to borrow money. I was in possession of nearly one hundred dollars at the time, and they were very destitute of provisions and comforts of life generally. Brother Young said he had nothing in his house to eat, and he knew not how to get anything. He said he had been standing in the door of the printing office thinking of his condition and felt so bad that the sweat rolled off of him. Soon Brother Parley came along, and he said to him, 'What shall we do I have nothing to eat, and I don't know how nor where to get it.' Brother Pratt said, 'There is a brother and his wife who have just arrived at my house, and he has got some money, and I think he will lend us some.' (I had lent Brother Pratt seven dollars before this.) So they all three came, and I lent them seventy five dollars; twenty-five for each, and they gave me their joint note" ("Autobiography," p. 16).

It appeared almost impossible that the commandment to build this temple could be fulfilled. Not only were the Saints poor, but their "enemies were raging and threatening destruction" upon them. "We had to guard ourselves night after night," Heber C. Kimball said, "and for weeks were not permitted to take off our clothes, and were obliged to lay with our fire locks in our arms" (*Times and Seasons*, 15 Jan. 1845, p. 771). Amid this poverty and persecution, Latter-day Saints realized that God would continue to aid them. "The Lord had promised [in D&C 64:21, given during the fall of 1831] to keep a stronghold in Kirtland for the space of five years; therefore," Joel Johnson testified, "we were warned of all the devices of our enemies in time to elude them until the temple was completed, the saints endowed and the five years expired" ("Autobiography," p. 5). The temple was dedicated in 1836 just before the promised five years ended.

17

CONFLICT IN JACKSON COUNTY

Doctrine and Covenants 97–101

Doctrine and Covenants 97, 98, and 101 were given in Ohio, but they are concerned more with events in Missouri.

COUNSEL TO THE PERSECUTED SAINTS

Early in July 1833 hundreds of the Saints' enemies, including some of the most prominent religious, political, and economic leaders of Jackson County, signed a "secret constitution," which Latter-day Saints called "the manifesto of the mob." This document ordered the Mormons immediately to close their merchandizing stores, discontinue printing operations, stop further immigration, and leave Jackson County. An unusual aspect of this document was a list of grievances that the mob used to justify its actions. The manifesto described the Latter-day Saints as "fanatics, or knaves, (for one or the other they undoubtedly are)" who pretend "to hold personal communication and converse face to face with the Most High God; to receive communications and revelations direct from heaven; to heal the sick by laying on hands; and, in short, to perform all the wonder-working miracles wrought by the inspired Apostles and Prophets of old." Therefore, they vowed to remove the Mormons from their society, "peaceably if we can, forcibly if we must" [History of the Church, 1:374–76].

According to Parley P. Pratt, when Latter-day Saint leaders refused to agree to the terms of the manifesto, "the mob met at the court house on the 20th of July, and proceeded immediately to demolish the brick printing office and dwelling house of W. W. Phelps & Co., and destroyed or took possession of the press, type, books and property of the establishment; — at the same time turning Mrs. Phelps and children out of doors: after which they proceeded to personal violence by a wanton assault and battery upon the Bishop of the church, Mr. Edward Partridge, and a Mr. [Charles] Allen, whom they tarred and feathered, and variously abused. They then compelled Messrs. Gilbert[,] Whitney & Co. to close their store and pack their goods" [*History of Persecution*, p. 7]. Copies of the nearly completed Book of Commandments were rescued courageously by two teenage Mormon girls (see Chapter 1).

When the Prophet received Doctrine and Covenants 97 and 98 about two weeks later in Ohio, he was not yet aware of how the mob had abused Church members and destroyed their property. Joseph could have known only by revelation that persecution had intensified. In these revelations, he was inspired to counsel the Saints not to neglect the temple, to be pure in heart, to renounce war, and refrain from seeking revenge.

THE SAINTS ARE EXPELLED
FROM JACKSON COUNTY

When the leaders of the Missourians learned that the Latter-day Saints would not comply with the terms of the "manifesto," mobs again attacked, burning homes and beating Saints. Governor Daniel Dunklin called out the militia to establish peace, but they seized only the Mormons' guns and allowed the Saints' enemies to renew their depredations. Finally, in early November 1833, approximately one thousand Latter-day Saints were driven by mobs from Jackson County. In one of the first accounts of events that had preceded the expulsion of Saints from Jackson County, Parley P. Pratt stated:

"On Friday, the first of November, women and children sallied forth from their gloomy retreats, to contemplate, with heart-rending anguish, the ravages of a ruthless mob, in the mangled bodies of their husbands, and in the destruction of their houses and furniture. Houseless, and unprotected by the arm of civil law in Jackson County—the dreary month of November staring them in the face, and loudly proclaiming a more inclement season at hand—the continual threats of the mob, that they would drive every Mormon from the county—and the inability of many to remove because of their poverty, caused an anguish of heart indescribable.

"These outrages were committed about two miles from my residence. News reached me before day-light the same morning, and I immediately repaired to the place, and was filled with anguish at the awful sight of houses in ruins, and furniture destroyed and strewed about the streets; women, in different directions, were weeping and mourning, while some of the men were covered with blood from the blows they had received from the enemy; others were endeavoring to collect the fragments of their scattered furniture, beds, &c. . . .

"The same night (Friday) a party in Independence commenced stoning houses, breaking down doors and windows, destroying furniture, &c. This night the brick part of a dwelling house belonging to A. S. Gilbert, was partly demolished, and the windows of his dwelling broken in, while a gentleman lay sick in his house.

"The same night, the doors of the house of Messrs. Gilbert & Whitney were split open, and the goods strewed in the street, to which fact upwards of twenty witnesses can attest.

"After midnight a party of our men marched for the store, &c., and when the mob saw them approach, they fled. But one of their number, a Richard McCarty, was caught in the act of throwing rocks in at the door, while the goods lay strung around him in the street. He was immediately taken before Samuel Weston, Esq. and a warrant requested, that said McCarty might be secured; but his justiceship refused to do any thing in the case, and McCarty was then liberated.

" . . . Saturday night a party of the mob made an attack upon a settlement about six miles west of town. Here they tore the roof from a dwelling, broke open another house, found the owner, Mr. David Bennett, sick in bed. Him they beat inhumanly, and swore they would blow his brains out, and discharging a pistol, the ball cut a deep gash across the top of his head. In this skirmish one of their men was shot in the thigh" (*History of Persecution*, pp. 8–9).

At least one miracle occurred during a battle between the Latter-day Saints and their enemies. Philo Dibble recounted being shot and bleeding inwardly until his body was filled with blood: "I was then examined by a surgeon who . . . said that he had seen a great many men wounded, but never saw one wounded as I was that ever lived. He pronounced me a dead man.

"David Whitmer, however, sent me word that I should live and not die, but I could see no possible chance to recover. After the surgeon had left me, Brother Newell Knight came to see me, and sat down on the side of my bed. He laid his right hand on my head, but never spoke. I felt the Spirit resting upon me at the crown of my head before his hand touched me, and I knew immediately that I was going to be healed. It seemed to form like a ring under the skin, and followed down my body. When the ring came to the wound, another ring formed around the first bullet hole, also the second and third. Then a ring formed on each shoulder and on each hip, and followed down to the ends of my fingers and toes and left me. I immediately arose and discharged three quarts of blood or more, with some pieces of my clothes that had been driven into my body by the bullets. I then dressed myself and . . . from that time not a drop of blood came from me and I never afterwards felt the slightest pain or inconvenience from my wounds, except that I was somewhat weak from the loss of blood" (*Faith Promoting Classics*, pp. 84–85).

A most descriptive account of the tragic exodus of the Saints from Jackson County was written by Parley P. Pratt: "Thursday, November 7th, the shore began to be lined on both sides of the ferry with men, women, children, goods, wagons, boxes, chests, provisions, &c., while the ferry men were very busily employed in crossing them over; and when night again closed upon us, the wilderness had much the appearance of a camp meeting. Hundreds of people were seen in every direction—some in tents and some in the open air, around their fires, while the rain descended in torrents. Husbands were inquiring for wives, and women for their husbands; parents for children, and children for parents. Some had had the good fortune to escape with their families, household goods and some provisions: while others knew not the fate of their friends, and had lost all their goods. The scene was indescribable" (*History of Persecution*, p. 12).

Orange Wight, the son of Lyman Wight, remembered that after crossing the Missouri River, some of his family camped near a big sycamore log six feet in diameter. He and others "laid a few poles on one side on the top of the log" and placed the other end on the ground. Then they spread a quilt or two on the poles. "Under the quilts and poles by the side of the big log" his brother, Lehi Lyman Wight, was born. At that time, he added, a mob was chasing his father, threatening to kill him, and the family was almost in a state of starvation. For three weeks the family lived in fear, not knowing the fate of their father. Orange testified that the Lord then answered their prayers. Their father evaded the mobs, crossed the river, and located his family. Meanwhile, one of the Church members, John Higbee, secured an old flintlock gun (Missourians had previously seized the guns of the Mormons) and shot eleven deer. Members also found wild bee trees. "Hence," Orange concluded, "we lived on venison and honey" ("Autobiography," pp. 1–2).

The Saints built temporary homes as best they could, searching out and making habitable all the old shanties and hovels that could be found, endeavoring to keep as close together as possible. Edward

Partridge and Elder John Corrill "procured an old log cabin that had been used for a stable and cleaned it up as best they could." The floor in this one-room cabin was nearly torn up, and Emily Partridge remembered that "the rats and rattlesnakes were too thick for comfort." Blankets were hung a few feet from the fireplace and the two families, fifteen or sixteen in number, gathered near the fire to keep from freezing. John Corrill's family occupied one side of the fireplace and Edward Partridge's the other. Emily added that "our beds were in the back part of the room" which reminded her of the "polar regions" (*Woman's Exponent*, 15 Feb. 1885, p. 138).

In December, after the Prophet learned of the expulsion, he inquired of the Lord and learned why the Lord had not intervened in the Saints' behalf. The Lord chastised the converts for their transgressions but assured them that he had not forgotten them. They still needed to prepare for the Millennium, and, through parables, the Lord told them what to do. The Saints were to maintain their interest in Missouri.

THE SAINTS' INTEREST IN ZION CONTINUES

The exiles crossed the Missouri River from Jackson County into Clay County, and most settled there. When the Latter-day Saints established schools, some of the earlier settlers of Clay County sent their children to attend classes there. "Of course," Emily Partridge wrote, these children "were better dressed than the Mormon children, which caused them to sometimes sneer and make fun of our shabby clothes, but generally we got along very well. The Saints were very poor, and I sometimes wonder how they provided for their families the necessaries of life. My father being Bishop made the times much harder for him, for he not only had his family to provide for, but he had the poor to look after and provide for their comfort also" (*Woman's Exponent*, 15 Feb. 1885, p. 138).

Not all of the Saints moved from Jackson County to Clay County. Thomas Marsh located in Lafayette County, where he taught school. Others went to Ray and Van Buren counties. "We scattered in every direction," one Saint wrote. After moving to Van Buren County, some members were invited to settle in Clay County, where they "were treated with the utmost kindness" (*Millennial Star*, 11 July 1881, p. 439).

The migration of Latter-day Saints from other states to western Missouri continued after the expulsion of the Mormons from Jackson

County. Edward Stevenson arrived in Clay County, a lonely teenaged boy from southern Michigan. Leaving what he referred to as a "desirable" situation—his mother, who had been recently widowed, owned a comfortable home and 240 acres of good land—he packed his belongings in a small box and, with only one dollar in his pocket, started walking alone toward Zion. He soon joined with other converts from Michigan who were heading to western Missouri and arranged with a family to drive their ox team. After arriving in Clay County, young Edward found himself alone amid strangers, but he was impressed with the new land. ("Autobiography," pp. 8–9).

In harmony with the Lord's counsel given in Doctrine and Covenants 101, Church members continued to gather in the Missouri frontier in anticipation of the day when Zion would be redeemed.

18

ZION'S CAMP: A TEST OF FAITH

Doctrine and Covenants 103; 105

After the Saints were driven from Jackson County, the Prophet was told that the governor of Missouri, Daniel Dunklin, would call out the militia to aid the Mormons in returning to their property if they would raise an army that could protect the people when the militia withdrew.

RECRUITING ZION'S CAMP

On 24 February 1834, Joseph Smith received a revelation regarding the redemption of Zion, meaning the restoration of the Saints to their lands in Jackson County. The Lord specified in this revelation the plan of organization and the minimum numerical strength of the army that would march to Missouri. He also warned the Saints that the "redemption of Zion" would come only after much tribulation and would be delayed if Church members continued to "pollute their inheritance." Nevertheless, the Lord promised, ultimately, when the Saints were worthy, his angels and his presence would go before them that they might "possess the goodly land" (D&C 103).

After two and one-half months of recruiting, Church leaders were disappointed that only one hundred men, the minimum number set by the Lord, enlisted. Nevertheless, the recruits prepared to march westward. George A. Smith, one of the youngest of the group, recorded: "On Sunday, May 4th, Joseph preached to the Saints in Kirtland, under the shade of the new school house, which was partially enclosed. Many of those who were to form the 'camp of Zion' being present, he impressed upon them the necessity of being humble, exercising faith and patience, and living in obedience to the commandments of the Almighty, and not murmur at the dispensations of Providence. He bore testimony of the truth of the work which God had revealed through him, and promised the brethren, that if they would all live as they should before the Lord, keeping

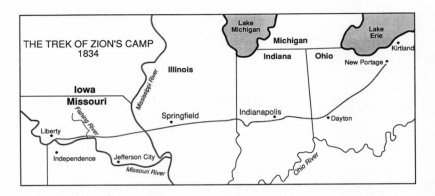

his commandments, and not like the Children of Israel murmur against the Lord and his servants, they should all safely return, and not one of them should fall upon the mission they were about to undertake" *(Millennial Star,* 15 July 1865, p. 439).

THE MARCH BEGINS

Many Kirtland Saints had mixed emotions and deep concerns as they left their families and friends to assist the afflicted in Missouri. Heber C. Kimball wrote: "We gathered clothing and other necessaries to carry up to our brethren and sisters who had been stripped; and putting our horses to the wagons, and taking our firelocks and ammunition, we started on our journey; leaving only Oliver Cowdery, Sidney Rigdon, and the workmen who were engaged at the Temple; so that there were very few men left in Kirtland. Our wagons were about full with baggage &c., consequently we had to travel on foot. We started on the 5th of May [1834], and truly this was a solemn morning to me. I took leave of my wife and children and friends, not expecting ever to see them again, as myself and brethren were threatened both in that country and in Missouri by the enemies, that they would destroy us and exterminate us from the land" *(Times and Seasons,* 15 Jan. 1845, p. 771).

The members of Zion's Camp gathered at New Portage, a community forty miles southwest of Kirtland. They were assigned responsibilities and, pooling their money, resumed their march on May 8.

In many respects, Zion's Camp was an unusual army. Called to action by revelation, the soldiers were led and instructed regularly by a modern prophet; they prayed frequently, and they were accompanied by heavenly messengers.

Parley P. Pratt rode his horse parallel with the army as he sought new volunteers. "On one occasion," he wrote, "I had travelled all night to overtake the camp with some men and means, and having breakfasted with them and changed horses, I again started ahead on express to visit other branches, and do business to again overtake them. At noon I had turned my horse loose from the carriage to feed on the grass in the midst of a broad, level plain. No habitation was near; stillness and repose reigned around me; I sank down overpowered with a deep sleep, and might have lain in a state of oblivion till the shades of night had gathered around me, so completely was I exhausted for want of sleep and rest; but I had only slept a few moments till the horse had grazed sufficiently, when a voice, more loud and shrill than I had ever before heard, fell on my ear, and thrilled through every part of my system; it said: *'Parley, it is time to be up and on your journey.'* In the twinkling of an eye I was perfectly aroused; I sprang to my feet so suddenly that I could not at first recollect where I was, or what was before me to perform. I related the circumstance afterwards to brother Joseph Smith, and he bore testimony that it was the angel of the Lord who went before the camp, who found me overpowered with sleep, and thus awoke me" *(Autobiography,* pp. 114–15).

Fearing persecution if others learned about the army's mission, Zion's Camp took various measures to conceal its identity. George A. Smith recorded:

"Tuesday, May 20. We traveled about 25 miles; part of the road being bad, and had to pull our wagons through the mud by ropes. We camped near Greenfield, Hancock County. While at dinner today three gentlemen came riding up on very fine-looking horses and commenced inquiring of various brethren concerning our traveling in so large a body, asking where we were from, and where we were going. The reply was, as usual, some from the State of Maine, some from [New] York State, some from Massachusetts, and some from Ohio, and others replied, 'We are from the East and as soon as we have done eating dinner, we shall be going to the West.' They then addressed themselves to Dr. [Frederick G.] Williams to see if they could find out who was the leader of the Camp. The Dr. replied, 'We have no one in particular.' 'But,' said they, 'is there not someone among you whom you call your captain or leader, or superior to the rest?' He answered, 'Sometimes one and sometimes another takes charge of the Company, so as not to throw the burden upon any one in particular.' These same spies who had come from the West passed us several times that day and the next, changing their horses and clothes and disguising themselves in various ways, yet we knew them.

"Wednesday, May 21. We traveled 28 miles, passing through Indianapolis and crossing White River. We had frequently been threatened that the Governor of Indiana would stop us at Indianapolis. This excited fear in the breasts of some of the company, in consequence of which Joseph directed as many as could to get into wagons and then drive some distance apart, the footmen scattering through different streets. In this manner we passed through the City unobserved by its inhabitants who were wondering when the great company they had heard of was going to pass. This fulfilled Joseph Smith's prediction to the fearful that we would not be interrupted. . . .

"Sunday, June 1. At half-past 10 this morning our trumpet, a common brass, French Horn, sounded in the Camp for preaching. There were some two or three hundred of the people from Jacksonville and the surrounding country gathered under the trees within our camp, and a chest was brought out for the accommodation of the speakers, when Squire Cook (Joseph Smith) took the stand professing to be a liberal free-thinker. He spoke to the people very freely about one hour on his particular views; his manner and style were very unassuming and affable, and he was listened to with great attention, and those present remarked that he was one of the greatest reasoners they ever heard" (*Instructor*, Mar. 1946, pp. 116–17, 182).

ZION'S CAMP IN MISSOURI

After arriving in eastern Missouri, Joseph's division was united with another group from Michigan and other northern states under Hyrum Smith's direction. The army now numbered more than two hundred men, plus a few women and children who were traveling with their husbands to Missouri. Elder Pratt rode ahead of Zion's Camp to Jefferson City and notified Governor Dunklin of the approaching army. Apparently fearing that any attempt to assist the Saints in regaining their land would lead to civil war, the governor, according to Elder Pratt, changed his mind and refused to call out the militia. The attempt to redeem Zion in 1834 was then postponed.

Nevertheless, the army continued its march toward Clay County, where most of the refugees lived.

One of the participants in this march, Nathan Baldwin, recalled the threat and the miracle at Fishing River: "As we neared our place of destination, the excitement of the people in the surrounding country increased. Many threats were thrown out against us but none were consummated. At an early hour at evening, on the 19th of June we encamped on an eminence between two forks of Fishing River, near a Baptist meeting house, built of hewn logs. While we busied ourselves preparing for the night, several armed men rode by (as we were camped on one side of the road) and swore that we should see hell before morning, and they told us of companies that were coming from various places, report said sixteen hundred sworn to our utter destruction. Soon after these men left, a small black cloud appeared in the west and increased in size until shortly the whole blue arch was draped in black, presenting a vengeful appearance, while the rain descended in torrents, the winds bellowed and such vivid flashes of lightning and such peals of thunder are seldom seen and heard.

"The Lord had previously said he would fight the battles of his saints, and it seemed as though the mandate had gone forth from his presence, to ply the artillery of heaven in defense of his servants. Some small hail fell in the camp but from half a mile to a mile around, we were told by the inhabitants that the hailstones were as big as tumblers; and the appearance of their destructiveness showed that their size was not over-estimated. Limbs of trees were broken off, fence rails were marred and splintered and the growing corn was cut into shreds. But the casualties were all on the side of our enemies. While their gathering hosts were hastening to our destruction, the wrathful elements met them in a manner they had not been accustomed to in their previous deeds of darkness, while persecuting the Saints. Thus brought to a sudden stand, they crept under trees, wagons and anything that afforded shelter and they held their horses as long as they could stand the pelting of these chunks of ice on their arms and gunstocks, the maddened steeds broke loose from the grasp and left them to face danger on foot, while their would-be victims were secure from harm, with the exception of some few tents which were blown down and a few men were rained on, but others were safely housed in the meeting house before mentioned. All were conscious that God was engaged in the conflict, and thankful that they were under his special care and kind protection.

"Next morning the streams before and behind us were wonderfully swollen so that we could not advance, neither could our enemies reach us if they had had a mind so to do, but it appears from the sequel that they were so dumbfounded by this singular defeat that their anxiety and determination to kill Jo Smith and his army was considerably abated, so much so that they were hardly willing to hazard another battle when Jehovah fights.

"We moved our camp four or five miles north to a more convenient location and halted for a few days. On Saturday the 21st [June 1834], Colonel Sconce with two other leading men from Ray County came to see us, desiring to know what our intentions were, for, said he, 'I see that there is an Almighty power that protects this people, for I started from Richmond, Ray County, with a company of armed men, having a full determination to destroy you, but was kept back by the storm and was not able to reach you.' When he entered our camp he was seized with such a trembling that he was obliged to sit down to compose himself before he made known the object of their visit. But when a proper explanation was made by Joseph the Prophet in a lengthy speech, they were melted into compassion and cordially took Joseph by the hand and promised to use their influence to allay the excitement of the people in the surrounding country, which they afterwards fulfilled by riding amongst the people and made unwearied exertions to that effect.

"The next day Cornelius Gillium, the sheriff of Clay County, came to the camp to hold a consultation. He was granted an audience and his first inquiries were if Joseph Smith was in camp, as he had heard he was, and if so he would like to see him. Whereupon Joseph arose and said, 'I am the man.' Mr. Gillium replied that he took him to be Mr. Smith but someone had told him that it was Captain Bruce. This was the first time that he had been made known to strangers since leaving Kirtland, having passed by several misnomers at different times. At first (and I suppose at his own instance) he was respectfully addressed as 'Esquire Cook', perhaps in consequence of his original name being Joseph Cook Smith, and discarding Cook at a more mature age.

"Mr. Gillium said the inhabitants were greatly excited in consequence of our appearance in the country and many inflammatory stories were told of us, amongst which was that the inscription on our banner was indicative of blood and carnage. Whereupon our flag was produced to his view, exhibiting a small white flag, right-angled triangle in shape, the extreme point tipped with red, and I think in large red letters was the word 'P E A C E'—the only letters on it.

"Mr. Gillium then gave some instructions concerning the manners, customs, and dispositions of the people, and what course would be policy for us to pursue in order to secure their favor and protection.

"On this ground was given the revelation [D&C 105:12–19] . . . in which we were told that God did not require at our hands to fight the battles of Zion. 'For,' said he, 'as I said in a former commandment, even so will I fulfill. I will fight your battles. But the strength of mine house has not hearkened unto my words, but inasmuch as there are those who have hearkened unto my words, I have prepared a blessing and an endowment for them, if they continue faithful. I have heard their prayers and will accept their offering; and it is expedient in me that they should be brought thus far, for a trial of their faith.' . . .

"This intelligence was the most acceptable to me of anything I had ever heard before, the gospel being the exception. But some of the camp was not pleased with it; and I think apostatized over it" ("Autobiography," pp. 12–14).

The dreaded disease of cholera tragically struck the members of Zion's Camp shortly before they arrived at Liberty. Seventy persons were afflicted, and of those, twelve soldiers and one woman died. In the midst of this illness, God's presence and intervention were again witnessed by the Saints, as testified by Wilford Woodruff: "After we had pitched our tents in Clay county . . . and many of the brethren had taken sick, and some had died, Joseph requested the camp to disperse, except enough to take care of the sick. All who had teams were required to leave the ground and go among the brethren. . . . Shortly, Joseph called the brethren together at Lyman Wight's, and told them if they would humble themselves before the Lord, and covenant to keep His commandments and obey His counsel, the plague should be stayed from that hour, and there should not be another case of cholera in the Camp. The brethren covenanted to do this, and the plague was stayed, and there was not another case in Camp" (*Millennial Star*, 25 Mar. 1865, p. 183).

Some critics regarded Zion's Camp as a failure because the army did not restore the Saints to their property in Jackson County. Nevertheless, the march strengthened the faith of the members of the camp, and from their number the original Quorums of Twelve and Seventy were called the following year. The Prophet declared,

"Brethren, some of you are angry with me, because you did not fight in Missouri; but let me tell you, God did not want you to fight. He could not organize His kingdom with twelve men to open the Gospel door to the nations of the earth, and with seventy men under their direction to follow in their tracks, unless He took them from a body of men who had offered their lives, and who had made as great a sacrifice as did Abraham" (*History of the Church,* 2:182 n.).

Other participants recognized the great influence that Zion's Camp had on their lives. "We gained an experience," Wilford Woodruff attested in December 1869, "that we never could have gained in any other way. We had the privilege of beholding the face of the prophet, and we had the privilege of travelling a thousand miles with him, and seeing the workings of the Spirit of God with him, and the revelations of Jesus Christ unto him and the fulfilment of those revelations" (*Journal of Discourses,* 13:158). President Brigham Young stated in October 1853: "When I returned from that mission to Kirtland, a brother said to me, 'Brother Brigham, what have you gained by this journey?' I replied, 'Just what we went for; but I would not exchange the knowledge I have received this season for the whole of Geauga County; for property and mines of wealth are not to be compared to the worth of knowledge' " (*Journal of Discourses,* 2:10).

19

VISIONS AND REVELATIONS DURING A PENTECOSTAL SEASON

Doctrine and Covenants 109–10; 137

During one of the greatest pentecostal seasons in the history of the Restoration, Joseph Smith received three visions or revelations that became Doctrine and Covenants 137, 109, and 110. Between 21 January and 1 May 1836, probably more Latter-day Saints beheld visions and witnessed other unusual spiritual manifestations than at any other period in the history of the Church. During ten meetings held in the Kirtland Temple, Latter-day Saints reported seeing angels and even the Savior. Some communed with heavenly messengers, many prophesied, some spoke in tongues, and some received the gift of interpretation of tongues.

Summarizing events that transpired during the dedication of the temple, Orson Pratt declared in 1875: "God was there, his angels were there, the Holy Ghost was in the midst of the people, the visions of the Almighty were opened to the minds of the servants of the living God; the vail was taken off from the minds of many; they saw the heavens opened; they beheld the angels of God; they heard the voice of the Lord; and they were filled from the crown of their heads to the soles of their feet with the power and inspiration of the Holy Ghost. . . .

"It was in that Temple that the visions of the Almighty were opened to our great Prophet, Seer and Revelator, Joseph Smith, wherein the future was portrayed before him, wherein keys were committed to him in relation to this great Latter-day dispensation, and the power of God was made manifest through the holy Priesthood sent down from heaven. In that Temple, set apart by the servants of God, and dedicated by a prayer that was written by inspiration, the people were blessed as they never had been blessed for generations and generations" (*Journal of Discourses*, 18:132).

A VISION OF THE CELESTIAL KINGDOM

Oliver Cowdery described one of the first meetings in the newly completed Kirtland Temple: "Thursday, the 21st [January 1836]. . . . At about three o'clock P.M. I assembled in our office garret, having all things prepared for the occasion, with Presidents Joseph Smith, jr., F. [Frederick] G. Williams, Sidney Rigdon, Hyrum Smith, David Whitmer, John Whitmer and elder John Corrill, and washed our bodies with pure water before the Lord, preparatory to the annointing with the holy oil. After we were washed, our bodies were perfumed with a sweet smelling oderous wash" (*BYU Studies*, Summer 1972, pp. 418–19).

The Prophet recorded: "We attended the ordinance of washing our bodies in pure water. We also perfumed our bodies and our heads, in the name of the Lord.

"At early candle-light I met with the Presidency at the west school room, in the Temple, to attend to the ordinance of anointing our heads with holy oil; also the Councils of Kirtland and Zion met in the two adjoining rooms, and waited in prayer while we attended to the ordinance. I took the oil in my left hand, Father Smith being seated before me, and the remainder of the Presidency encircled him round about. We then stretched our right hands towards heaven, and blessed the oil, and consecrated it in the name of Jesus Christ.

"We then laid our hands upon our aged Father Smith, and invoked the blessings of heaven. I then anointed his head with the consecrated oil, and sealed many blessings upon him. The Presidency then in turn laid their hands upon his head, beginning at the oldest, until they had all laid their hands upon him, and pronounced such blessings upon his head, as the Lord put into their hearts, all blessing him to be our Patriarch, to anoint our heads, and attend to all duties that pertain to that office. The Presidency then took the seat in their turn, according to their age, beginning at the oldest, and received their anointing and blessing under the hands of Father Smith. And in my turn, my father anointed my head, and sealed upon me the blessings of Moses, to lead Israel in the latter days, even as Moses led him in days of old; also the blessings of Abraham, Isaac and Jacob. All of the Presidency laid their hands upon me, and pronounced upon my head many prophecies and blessings, many of which I shall not notice at this time. But as Paul said, so say I, let us come to visions and revelations" (*History of the Church*, 2:379–80).

The Prophet quoted what is now Doctrine and Covenants 137 and then gave an account of yet another vision:

"I saw the Twelve Apostles of the Lamb, who are now upon the earth, who hold the keys of this last ministry, in foreign lands, standing together in a circle, much fatigued, with their clothes tattered and feet swollen, with their eyes cast downward, and Jesus standing in their midst, and they did not behold Him. The Savior looked upon them and wept.

"I also beheld Elder M'Lellin in the south, standing upon a hill, surrounded by a vast multitude, preaching to them, and a lame man standing before him supported by his crutches; he threw them down at his word and leaped as a hart, by the mighty power of God. Also, I saw Elder Brigham Young standing in a strange land, in the far south and west, in a desert place, upon a rock in the midst of about a dozen men of color, who appeared hostile. He was preaching to them in their own tongue, and the angel of God standing above his head, with a drawn sword in his hand, protecting him, but he did not see it. And I finally saw the Twelve in the celestial kingdom of God. I also beheld the redemption of Zion, and many things which the tongue of man cannot describe in full.

"Many of my brethren who received the ordinance with me saw glorious visions also. Angels ministered unto them as well as to myself, and the power of the Highest rested upon us, the house was filled with the glory of God, and we shouted Hosanna to God and the Lamb. My scribe also received his anointing with us, and saw, in a vision, the armies of heaven protecting the Saints in their return to Zion, and many things which I saw.

"The Bishop of Kirtland with his Counselors, and the Bishop of Zion with his Counselors, were present with us, and received their anointings under the hands of Father Smith, and this was confirmed by the Presidency, and the glories of heaven were unfolded to them also.

"We then invited the High Councilors of Kirtland and Zion into our room, and President Hyrum Smith anointed the head of the President of the Councilors in Kirtland, and President David Whitmer the head of the President of the Councilors of Zion. The President of each quorum then anointed the heads of his colleagues, each in his turn, beginning at the oldest.

"The visions of heaven were opened to them also. Some of them saw the face of the Savior, and others were ministered unto by holy angels, and the spirit of prophecy and revelation was poured out in mighty power; and loud hosannas, and glory to God in the highest, saluted the heavens, for we all communed with the heavenly host. And I saw in my vision all of the Presidency in the celestial kingdom of God, and many others that were present. Our meeting was opened by singing, and prayer was offered up by the head of each quorum; and closed by singing, and invoking the benediction of heaven, with uplifted hands. Retired between one and two o'clock in the morning" (*History of the Church*, 2:381–82).

Oliver Cowdery summarized the spiritual manifestations that took place during that meeting. He pointed out that the brethren "were annointed with the same kind of oil and in the man[ner] that were Moses and Aaron. . . . The glorious scene is too great to be described in this book, therefore, I only say, that the heavens were opened to many, and great and marvelous things were shown" (*BYU Studies*, Summer 1972, p. 419).

The apostles and the presidents of the seventy received their anointing the next day, after which many saw heavenly beings, members were blessed with the gift of tongues, and, as Joseph said, "angels mingled their voices with ours" (*History of the Church*, 2:383).

The spiritual manifestations continued. On Thursday, 28 January, during the meeting in which the Prophet "attended to the sealing of what they had done," Zebedee Coltrin saw the Savior, others beheld heavenly beings, and Joseph saw "a glorious vision" (*History of the Church*, 2:387). On Saturday, 6 February, the Prophet called all who had been anointed "together to receive the seal of all their blessings." Many who were obedient to his instructions received unusual blessings. Some saw visions. "Others were filled with the Spirit" and spoke in tongues, and some prophesied. "This was a time of rejoicing long to be remembered," Joseph said (*History of the Church*, 2:391–92).

THE LORD'S HOUSE IS DEDICATED

On Saturday, 26 March, Church leaders met in the president's room to prepare for the dedication of the Lord's house. The Prophet, directed by the Lord and assisted by others, including Oliver Cowdery, wrote the prayer for the dedication of the temple, now recorded in Doctrine and Covenants 109 (*BYU Studies*, Summer 1972, p. 426).

On the following day, Sunday, 27 March, the temple was dedicated, and Latter-day Saints experienced a spiritual feast. "The dedication was looked forward to with intense interest," Eliza R. Snow remembered, "and when the day arrived . . . a dense multitude assembled—the temple was filled to its utmost, and when the ushers were compelled to close the doors, the outside congregation was nearly if not quite as large as that within.

"Four hundred and sixteen elders, including prophets and apostles, with the first great prophets of the last dispensation at their head, were present—men who had been 'called of God as was Aaron,' and clothed with the holy priesthood; many of them having just returned from missions, on which they had gone forth like the ancient disciples, 'without purse or scrip,' now to feast for a little season on the sweet spirit of love and union, in the midst of those who had 'tasted of the powers of the world to come.'

"At the hour appointed, the assembly was seated. . . . At nine o'clock, President Sidney Rigdon commenced the services of that great and memorable day, by reading the ninety-sixth and twenty-fourth Psalms; 'Ere long the vail will be rent in twain,' etc., was sung by the choir, and after President Rigdon had addressed the throne of grace in fervent prayer, 'O happy souls who pray,' etc., was sung. President Rigdon then read the eighteenth, nineteenth, and twentieth verses of the eighteenth chapter of Matthew, and spoke more particularly from the last-named verse, continuing his eloquent, logical and sublime discourse for two and a half hours. At one point, as he reviewed the toils and privations of those who had labored in rearing the walls of that sacred edifice, he drew tears from many eyes . . .

"He admitted there were many houses—many sufficiently large, built for the worship of God, but not one, except this, on the face of the whole earth, that was built by divine revelation; and were it not for this, the dear Redeemer might, in this day of science, intelligence and religion, say to those who would follow him, 'The foxes have holes, the birds of the air have nests, but the Son of Man hath not where to lay his head.'

"After the close of his discourse, President Rigdon presented for an expression of their faith and confidence, Joseph Smith, Jr., as prophet, seer and revelator, to the various quorums, and the whole congregation of saints, and a simultaneous rising up followed, in token of unanimous confidence, and covenant to uphold him as such, by their faith and prayers.

"The morning services were concluded by the choir singing,

'Now let us rejoice in the day of salvation,' etc. During an intermission of twenty minutes, the congregation remained seated, and the afternoon services opened by singing, 'This earth was once a garden place.' " Following the sustaining of Church leaders the dedicatory prayer was offered by Joseph Smith. . . .

"The choir then sang, 'The spirit of God like a fire is burning,' etc., after which the Lord's supper was administered to the whole assembly. Then President Joseph Smith bore testimony of his mission and of the ministration of angels, and, after testimonials and exhortations by other elders, he blest the congregation in the name of the Lord.

"Thus ended the ceremonies of the dedication of the first temple built by special command of the Most High, in this dispensation.

"One striking feature of the ceremonies, was the grand shout of hosanna, which was given by the whole assembly, in standing position, with uplifted hands. The form of the shout is as follows: 'Hosanna — hosanna — hosanna — to God and the Lamb — amen — amen, and amen.' The foregoing was deliberately and emphatically pronounced, and three times repeated, and with such power as seemed almost sufficient to raise the roof from the building.

"A singular incident in connection with this shout may be discredited by some, but it is verily true. A notice had been circulated that children in arms would not be admitted at the dedication of the temple. A sister who had come a long distance with her babe six weeks old, having, on her arrival, heard of the above requisition, went to the patriarch Joseph Smith, Sr., in great distress, saying that she knew no one with whom she could leave her infant; and to be deprived of the privilege of attending the dedication seemed more than she could endure. The ever generous and kind-hearted father volunteered to take the responsibility on himself, and told her to take her child, at the same time giving the mother a promise that her babe should make no disturbance; and the promise was verified. But when the congregation shouted hosanna, that babe joined in the shout. As marvelous as that incident may appear to many, it is not more so than other occurrences on that occasion.

"The ceremonies of that dedication may be rehearsed, but no mortal language can describe the heavenly manifestations of that memorable day. Angels appeared to some, while a sense of divine presence was realized by all present and each heart was filled with 'joy inexpressible and full of glory' " (Tullidge, *Women of Mormondom*, 82–95).

In the evening following the dedication, priesthood leaders experienced another unusual service. "The Spirit was poured out," Oliver Cowdery recounts, and "I saw the glory of God, like a great cloud, come down and rest upon the house, and fill the same like a mighty rushing wind. I also saw cloven tongues, like as of fire rest upon many, (for there were 316 present,) while they spake with other tongues and prophesied" (*BYU Studies*, Summer 1972, p. 426).

Although the temple ordinances as we know them today were not performed at Kirtland, keys of the priesthood, including those related to temple service, were restored in that house of the Lord. On Easter Sunday, just one week after the temple was dedicated, four glorious messengers appeared there. The last entry in Joseph Smith's 1835–36 Kirtland Diary described the setting and the vision in which Christ accepted the sacrifices of the Saints, and Moses, Elias and Elijah restored priesthood keys (see D&C 110).

SPIRITUAL MANIFESTATIONS CONTINUE

Spiritual manifestations continued after the dedicatory services. "In Kirtland . . . we enjoyed many very great blessings, and often saw the power of God manifested," Prescindia Huntington wrote. "On one occasion I saw angels clothed in white walking upon the temple. It was during one of our monthly fast meetings, when the saints were in the temple worshipping. A little girl came to my door and in wonder called me out, exclaiming, 'The meeting is on the top of the meeting house!' I went to the door, and there I saw on the temple angels clothed in white covering the roof from end to end. They seemed to be walking to and fro; they appeared and disappeared. The third time they appeared and disappeared before I realized that they were not mortal men. Each time in a moment they vanished, and their reappearance was the same. This was in broad daylight, in the afternoon. A number of the children in Kirtland saw the same.

"When the brethren and sisters came home in the evening, they told of the power of God manifested in the temple that day, and of the prophesying and speaking in tongues. It was also said, in the interpretation of tongues, 'That the angels were resting down upon the house.'

"At another fast meeting I was in the temple with my sister Zina. The whole of the congregation were on their knees, praying vocally, for such was the custom at the close of these meetings when Father Smith presided; yet there was no confusion; the voices of the congregation mingled softly together. While the congregation was thus praying, we both heard, from one corner of the room above our heads, a choir of angels singing most beautifully. They were invisible to us, but myriads of angelic voices seemed to be united in singing some song of Zion, and their sweet harmony filled the temple of God" (Tullidge, *Women of Mormondom*, pp. 207–8).

When Nancy Tracy later reflected on her spiritual experiences in Kirtland, she observed that such remarkable manifestations would not continue. Nevertheless, she suggested that these blessings had prepared Latter-day Saints for the trials that awaited them. "We have the opposing element to contend with," and we "shall be made perfect through [our] suffering" ("Autobiography," p. 9).

20

THE SAINTS MOVE TO NORTHERN MISSOURI
Doctrine and Covenants 113–16

Seven revelations in our Doctrine and Covenants were recorded by the Prophet at Far West, Missouri, in 1838. Three were received in March or April (sections 113–15), and four more (117–20) were given in July. Most of the Saints living in Clay and surrounding counties had moved to the less populated sections in the northern part of Missouri because of increasing mob threats. The legislature responded to the large migration into northern Ray County by creating two new counties — Caldwell and Daviess. Far West, in newly created Caldwell County, became the principal gathering place by 1837, and from there Bishop Edward Partridge continued to direct the financial affairs of the Church. The Prophet left Ohio and located in Far West early in 1838. Another gathering place in Daviess County was named Adam-ondi-Ahman in a revelation received in May 1838 (D&C 116).

THE SAINTS BUILD FAR WEST

Bishop Partridge's daughter Emily recalled her family's move from Clay County to northern Missouri: "Father moved his family into a piece of timber, about three miles from the place where Far West was afterwards located. Father and the brethren that were with him built log huts and prepared us as well as they could for the coming winter. The timber in which we were camped was mostly hickory, with some black walnut, and hazle bushes were plentiful, and all were loaded with nuts, and when the frost came they dropped from the trees and lay so thick on the ground all around us that the children were kept pretty busy gathering them up. We gathered several bushels, and feasted on nuts through the winter, if with little else. As father's eldest children were all girls, my sister Harriet and I had to act the part of boys and help him with his work, such as milking the cows and going to the prairie and assist him in loading hay, and sometimes we would carry the chain when he surveyed the land.

"After Far West was laid out father built another house and we moved into the city. The Saints from all parts of the world, where the Gospel had been preached, began to gather in, and the place was rapidly built up" (*Woman's Exponent,* 15 June 1885, p. 10).

The Prophet Joseph Smith described the background of his move to Missouri from Ohio: as "a new year [1838] dawned upon the Church in Kirtland," the "spirit of apostate mobocracy" raged until he was "obliged to flee from its deadly influence, as did the Apostles and Prophets of old." Quoting the Savior, the Prophet said that "when they persecute you in one city, flee to another." On the night of 12 January 1838, Joseph Smith and Sidney Rigdon fled Kirtland, Ohio, to escape persecution. Joseph went to Far West, Missouri, and during the ensuing seven months, nearly all the Saints in Kirtland (more than sixteen hundred) were also forced to abandon their homes and their temple.

After a "long and tedious journey," Joseph Smith and his family arrived at Far West, Missouri, on 14 March 1838. Many Saints gathered to meet his family and welcomed them "with open arms." Two or three days later, his brother Samuel arrived with his family, and while the Prophet was "walking with him and certain other brethren," the "sentiments occurred to [his] mind" that were recorded as Doctrine and Covenants 113, which is the Prophet's answers to questions on scripture (*History of the Church,* 3:9).

The following month, Joseph received two revelations. One was for David Patten (D&C 114), calling him on a mission the following spring, but he was killed in October 1838, one of the casualties of the battle of Crooked River. In the other revelation (D&C 115), the Lord identified the official name of the Church. When the Church was organized in 1830, it was called the "Church of Christ." That name created problems for early missionaries because many churches and congregations employed this same name. To identify the movement led by the Prophet Joseph Smith, members began referring to their church as the Church of the Latter-day Saints. The revelation at Far West resolved this problem (*History of the Church,* 3:24 n.). But the main thrust of the Lord's instructions in Doctrine and Covenants 115 was to build up Far West.

Every family that arrived along the northern Missouri frontier faced similar challenges. Mosiah Hancock, son of Levi and Clarissa, remembered traveling from Ohio to Missouri in the spring of 1838, when he was four years old. Because his parents' wagon was so loaded with goods, he walked during most of the journey westward. He was barefoot during that trip; in fact, he "never knew the luxury of having a pair of shoes until I was seven years of age, then my Uncle Allah made me a present of a pair." He further remembered that when the family arrived near Plum Creek towards the end of March 1838, there were "approximately eight inches of snow on the ground, and not having a tent we were forced to camp in the open for awhile." He also recalled that one night he slept in a bed with sixteen other children. Most of the time during that late spring, however, he slept on the ground while his grandfather and grandmother and some of the children slept in a wagon.

Shortly after their arrival, the family built a log home. "The house," Mosiah wrote, "was daubed inside with clay, and chinked and daubed outside. Shakes were put on the roof; and a chimney was laid up of sticks and daubed inside and outside with clay mud. A pinion-floor was made. A bedstead was made out of tree limbs and posts so that mother might be as comfortable as possible while her baby was being born."

Mosiah Hancock also remembered experiences in Missouri with Joseph Smith: "It was the disposition of the Prophet Joseph when he saw little children in the mud to take them up in his arms and wash the mud from their bare feet with his handkerchief. And oh how kind he was to the old folks as well as to little children. He always had a smile for his friends and was always cheerful" ("Autobiography," pp. 3–4).

David Osborn, another convert who gathered with the Saints in Missouri, met Joseph Smith for the first time during a visit to Far West in 1838. "There were but three houses in town at that time," he wrote. "On the south side of the elder Peter Whitmer's house was a wagon with a box on [it]. Here were seated Joseph, Sidney Rigdon and others. There was quite a congregation including old residents (Gentiles) of Caldwell County. I remember many of his sayings. . . . Said he, 'You have heard many reports about me. Some perhaps are true and others not true. I know what I have done and I know what I have not done. . . . You may hug up to yourselves the Bible, but except through faith in it you can get revelation for yourself, the Bible will profit you but little. . . . The Book of Mormon is true, just what it purports to be, and for this testimony I expect to give an account in the day of judgment. . . . If I obtain the glory which I have in view I expect to wade through much tribulation.' "

"In closing his remarks the Prophet asserted, 'The Savior declared the time was coming when secret or hidden things should be revealed on the house tops. Well,' says he, 'I have revealed to you a few things, if not on the house top, on the wagon top' " (*Juvenile Instructor*, 15 Mar. 1892, p. 173).

Primarily as a result of increased immigration, the Latter-day Saint population continued to swell in 1838. The price of land increased sharply, and some members became involved in land speculation. Recognizing that many Latter-day Saints had made great sacrifices to move to Missouri, the Prophet did not approve of Church members making unusual profits at the expense of the new immigrants. Edward Stevenson noted that in 1838 high councils and bishop's courts were active in disciplining members not only for speculation but for disobeying the Word of Wisdom. He also stated that many small stores were then in operation, and dealers in intoxicants and tobacco were frowned upon and their businesses were not considered "legitimate" ("Autobiography," p. 24).

ADAM-ONDI-AHMAN

Doctrine and Covenants 116 is a selection from Joseph Smith's history added to the Doctrine and Covenants in 1876 that identifies a place near Wight's Ferry at Spring Hill in Daviess County, Missouri, as a site where Adam lived and will visit in the future. As Latter-day Saints sought new areas for expansion during the spring of 1838, the Prophet traveled northward:

"Friday, May 18[,1838]. — I left Far West . . . with . . . many others, for the purpose of visiting the north country, and laying off a stake of Zion; making locations, and laying claim to lands to facilitate the gathering of the Saints, and for the benefit of the poor, in upholding the Church of God. We traveled to the mouth of Honey Creek, which is a tributary of Grand river, where we camped for the night. We passed through a beautiful country the greater part of which is prairie, and thickly covered with grass and weeds, among which is plenty of game, such as deer, turkey, and prairie hen. . . .

"Saturday, 19. — This morning we struck our tents and formed a line of march, crossing Grand River at the mouth of Honey Creek and Nelson's Ferry. Grand River is a large, beautiful, deep and rapid stream, during the high waters of Spring, and will undoubtedly admit of navigation by steamboat and other water craft. At the mouth of Honey Creek is a good landing. We pursued our course up the river, mostly through timber, for about eighteen miles, when we arrived at Colonel Lyman Wight's home. He lives at the foot of Tower Hill (a name I gave the place in consequence of the remains of an old Nephite altar or tower that stood there), where we camped for the Sabbath.

"In the afternoon I went up the river about half a mile to Wight's Ferry, accompanied by President Rigdon, and my clerk, George W. Robinson, for the purpose of selecting and laying claim to a city plat near said ferry in Daviess County . . . which the brethren called 'Spring Hill,' but by the mouth of the Lord it was named Adam-ondi-Ahman, because, said He, it is the place where Adam shall come to visit his people, or the Ancient of Days shall sit, as spoken of by Daniel the Prophet [D&C 116]. . . .

"Monday, 21. . . . In the evening, I called a council of the brethren, to know whether it was wisdom to go immediately into the north country, or tarry here and hereabouts, to secure land on Grand River, etc. The brethren spoke their minds freely on the subject, when I stated to the council that I felt impressed to tarry and secure all the land near by, that is not secured between this and Far West, especially on Grand River. President Rigdon concurred, and the council voted unanimously to secure the land on Grand River, and between this and Far West" (*History of the Church*, 3:34–36).

In the summer of 1838, Latter-day Saints began settling Adam-ondi-Ahman. Lyman Wight's son, Orange Wight, remembered that his family was one of the first to move to the community that had been identified by Joseph Smith as a place where Adam had offered a holy sacrifice.

Orange Wight also remembered occasions when Joseph Smith and Sidney Rigdon visited his family. Joseph "was very kind and sociable with both young and old. We often bathed in the limpid waters of Grand River. Although but a boy I was invited to bathe with them. . . . We had a jolly time. . . . There was Joseph the Prophet, my father, Sidney Rigdon and several others. Our amusement consisted in part [of] seeing Brother Rigdon swim. He was so corpulent that he was forced to lay on his back to swim, he would swim in that way until his shoulders would strike the sand bar. Then he would turn but would flop back in deep water" ("Autobiography," p. 4).

Eliza R. Snow was another early settler of Adam-ondi-Ahman. She remembered that the old settlers placed "an embargo on all of the flouring mills" in that area, preventing the Latter-day Saints from obtaining meal they desired. "Our father had abundance of wheat, but could get no grinding. In this dilemma we had to resort to graters, made by perforating tin pails and stovepipes, on which we grated corn for bread material" (*Biography,* pp. 41–42).

About the middle of October 1838, Edward Stevenson visited Adam-ondi-Ahman and later recalled a conversation with the Prophet about that sacred site:

"The Prophet said it had been manifested unto him that here [Jackson County] was where our Father Adam was placed, and where his home was until his fall, when he was driven out into the dreary world, and from thence he took his departure northeast about seventy miles, to where a stake of Zion was located, and it was named Adam-Ondi-Ahman by revelation. This knowledge makes this land, which is good and greatly blessed, all the more attractive to the Saints, and creates a desire to cherish . . . the memory of the land. . . .

" . . . I was with the Prophet Joseph Smith . . . [and] others on the hill Adam-Ondi-Ahman. The Prophet said, pointing to a mound of stones:

" 'There is where Father Adam built an altar when he was driven from the Garden of Eden and offered up sacrifice unto the Lord.'

"He further said that the Garden of Eden was in or near Independence, the center stake of Zion. I thought it a great privilege to be at that time with the Prophet, and to hear his words regarding the mound and pile of rocks laid up at so early a period of the world's history" (*Reminiscences of Joseph,* pp. 40–41).

21

THE SAINTS MOVE TO FAR WEST

Doctrine and Covenants 117–20

At a conference in Far West, Missouri, on 8 July 1838, Joseph Smith not only presented for the first time three revelations he had received the day before fleeing from Kirtland (none of which are in our Doctrine and Covenants) but also received four more revelations, which are recorded in Doctrine and Covenants 117 through 20 *(History of the Church,* 3:44). These revelations were unfolded during a period of celebration and spiritual rejuvenation. Five days earlier, "on 3 July 1838 there was a general meeting of the Saints in Far West, [and] about 1500 met and had a grand time. Ground was broken for a temple, 110 feet by 80 feet, a house of the Lord to be reared in this, our day, and on this holy land once occupied by our father Adam. It seems like a dream almost to me that I should be so favored to be one of this most happy and favored assemblage for it is fresh to my mind and especially on the following day, the honored 4th of July. Several Missourians manifested their independence by being baptized into the Church of Jesus Christ of Latter-day Saints" (Edward Stevenson, "Autobiography," pp. 24–25).

The celebration continued on July 4. Early in the morning the Saints erected a "liberty pole" made from the largest tree they could find in the surrounding forest. The Stars and Stripes fluttered from the top. Joseph Smith recalled: "The day was spent in celebrating the Declaration of Independence of the United States of America, and also by the Saints making a 'Declaration of Independence' from all mobs and persecutions which have been inflicted upon them, time after time, until they could bear it no longer; having been driven by ruthless mobs and enemies of truth from their homes, and having had their property confiscated, their lives exposed, and their all jeopardized by such barbarous conduct. The corner stones of the House of the Lord, agreeable to the commandments of the Lord unto us, given April 26, 1838 [D&C 115:10], were laid" *(History of the*

Church, 3:41). Under the waving folds of the banner of freedom, the Latter-day Saints laid the cornerstone of a temple of God and dedicated the land and themselves and their families to Him who had preserved them in all their troubles.

Sidney Rigdon then addressed the Saints. He reminded them of the suffering they had endured at the hands of their enemies. He reminded them of their constitutional rights as American citizens and expressed a determination to resist, from that time forth, all oppression. He concluded by urging the Saints to maintain their rights and freedom, "according to the holy principles of liberty, as guaranteed to every person by the Constitution and laws of our country" (Pratt, *Autobiography,* p. 173).

SETTLING FINANCIAL AFFAIRS IN KIRTLAND

After the Independence Day celebrations, Church leaders directed a three-day conference beginning 6 July. On the final day of the conference, 8 July, the Prophet received four revelations. The Lord instructed William Marks and Newel K. Whitney to settle promptly their business affairs in Kirtland and move to Missouri. Because most of the Saints had already left Kirtland, and many were traveling westward in a group known as Kirtland Camp, the Prophet undoubtedly learned by revelation that these two men had tarried. Consequently, they were commanded to repent of their "covetous desires" and journey "from the land of Kirtland" before it snowed (D&C 117:1–5). Meanwhile, Oliver Granger was called on a mission to settle Church "business affairs" in Ohio. Joseph Smith explained, "As I was driven from Kirtland without the privilege of settling up my business, I . . . employed Colonel Oliver Granger as my agent, to close all my affairs in the east." In fleeing from mobs in Kirtland, Joseph had left debts and was accused of "running away" and "cheating [his] creditors" (*History of the Church,* 3:164). Oliver Granger sought contributions, collected money, moved to Kirtland, and attempted to pay all debts that Joseph had contracted on behalf of the Church.

A MISSION FOR THE TWELVE

During the July conference, the Prophet sought direction concerning the Twelve. Four of the original members of that quorum had been excommunicated (William E. McLellin, Luke S. Johnson, John F. Boynton, and Lyman E. Johnson), and four were called by revelation (D&C 118) to fill those vacancies. Another vacancy was created when David W. Patten was killed in the Battle of Crooked River. Twenty-year-old George A. Smith, who was called to fill that position, described how he first learned of his appointment.

"About the first of February I ascertained by accident that Brothers Brigham Young and Heber C. Kimball were going to Liberty to visit the prisoners [including the Prophet; see Chapter 22]. As they mounted their horses I joined them and asked permission to accompany them, which was readily granted. . . . I felt delicate about asking them for the privilege of accompanying them. On the way, Brother Kimball told me I was named to be one of the Twelve. . . .

"We traveled . . . to Liberty, and put up at a hotel, and waited until the victuals were carried in towards evening to the prisoners, when Judge [Samuel] Tillery, the Jailer, permitted us to go in and see the prisoners. We were locked in with them for about an hour. Joseph told me of my calling to the Apostleship and inquired how I liked it. I replied, 'I was pleased with the appointment, and would do my best to honor it.' He spent most of the time conversing with Brothers Brigham and Heber, and I have always regarded it as a blessing that I had the privilege of being locked up with those who were imprisoned for the kingdom of heaven's sake, if it was but for an hour" (*Instructor*, Mar. 1947, pp. 119, 142).

Doctrine and Covenants 118 also directed the Twelve to meet at Far West on 26 April 1839, the day construction on the temple was to resume, and depart from there "to go over the great waters" to serve a mission in Great Britain (compare D&C 118:4–5 with D&C 115:11). Because the Saints had been driven from Missouri during the winter of 1838–39 under threat of extermination, many of their enemies boasted that none of the Twelve would dare return to Far West on the appointed date—thus making Joseph Smith a false prophet. The Twelve themselves had mixed feelings about returning. John Taylor noted that they would have to "go among a people that would kill everyone of us as quick as they would rattlesnakes" (*Journal of Discourses*, 24:198). Under these conditions, some of the Apostles felt that the Lord would excuse them from going back to Missouri. Nevertheless, in the spirit of his new calling as president of the Quorum of the Twelve, Brigham Young determined that they would fulfill the Lord's commandment literally.

"Early on the morning of the 26th of April [1839], we held our Conference, cut off 31 persons from the Church and proceeded to the building spot of the Lord's House, where Elder Cutler, the master workman of the house, then re-commenced laying the foundation agreeably to revelation, by rolling up a large stone near the southeast corner. . . .

"[We] proceeded to ordain Wilford Woodruff and George A. Smith to the office of the Twelve, to fill the places of those who had fallen. . . .

"The Twelve then offered up vocal prayer . . . after which we sung 'Adam-ondi-Ahman,' and then we took our leave of the following Saints, agreeably to the revelation." After the meeting, Theodore Turley, who had accompanied the apostles to Far West, knocked on the door of Isaac Russell, one of the apostates who had insisted that the Twelve would not show up on the appointed date. "His wife answered, 'Come in — it is Brother Turley.' Russell replied, 'It is not; he left here two weeks ago,' and appeared quite alarmed; but on finding it was Turley, asked him to sit down; but he replied, 'I cannot; I shall lose my company.' 'Who is your company?' inquired Russell. 'The Twelve.' *'The Twelve?'* 'Yes; don't you know that this is the twenty-sixth, and the day the Twelve were to take leave of their friends on the foundation of the Lord's House, to go to the islands of the sea? The revelation is now fulfilled, and I am going with them.' Russell was speechless, and Turley bid him farewell.

"Thus was this revelation fulfilled, concerning which our enemies said, if all other revelations of Joseph Smith were fulfilled that one should not, as it had day and date to it" (*Millennial Star*, 12 Sept. 1863, pp. 583–84).

Nine of the Twelve responded to the call and went on their mission to Great Britain. Wilford Woodruff later described the success of their labors: "We went to England, and we baptized, in the year 1840, something like seven thousand people, and established churches in almost all the principal cities in the kingdom. Brother Pratt established a branch in Edinburgh, Scotland. Brother Kimball, George A. and myself built up a branch in London, and several branches in the south of England. We baptized eighteen hundred persons in the south of England in seven months; out of that number two hundred were preachers belonging to different denominations of that land. We opened an emigration office, published the Book of Mormon and gathered many to Zion. God was with us, and I may say that He has been in all the labors of this Church and kingdom" (*Journal of Discourses*, 13:160).

THE LAW OF TITHING

Finances became an increasing problem for the Church as the Saints settled in their new homes in northern Missouri. In fact, Bishop Partridge had personally assumed responsibility for a thousand dollars in Church expenses. Consequently, during the spring of 1838, Church leaders were giving attention to ways of raising funds. Tithing was one idea they considered.

The Prophet went to the Lord: "O Lord! Show unto thy servant how much thou requirest of the properties of thy people for a tithing?" The third revelation received on 8 July 1838, now Doctrine and Covenants 119, came in response. This revelation he "read to the public" (*History of the Church*, 3:44). Because the people had been living the law of consecration, in which they were to give a surplus each year, the revelation directed them first to fulfill this responsibility as the "beginning of the tithing of my people" and then to contribute one tenth of their income thereafter (D&C 119:3–4). On that same day, Joseph received a fourth revelation (D&C 120) relating to the disposition of properties received as tithes.

Brigham Young spoke of the Saints' varying acceptance of the law of tithing: "The brethren wished me to go among the Churches, and find out what surplus property the people had, with which to forward the building of the Temple we were commencing at Far West....

" ... I found the people said they were willing to do about as they were counselled, but, upon asking them about their surplus property, most of the men who owned land and cattle would say, 'I have got so many hundred acres of land, and I have got so many boys, and I want each one of them to have eighty acres, therefore this is not surplus property.' ... It is a laughable idea, but is nevertheless true, men would tell me they were young and beginning the world, and would say, 'We have no children, but our prospects are good, and we think we shall have a family of children, and if we do, we want to give them eighty acres of land each; we have no surplus property.' ...

" ... You would once in a while find a man who had a horse that he considered surplus, but at the same time he had the ringbone, was broken-winded, spavined in both legs, had the pole evil at one end of the neck and a fistula at the other, and both knees sprung.

"This is the description of surplus property that some would offer to the Lord" (*Journal of Discourses*, 2:306–7).

22

REVELATIONS FROM
A PRISON-TEMPLE

Doctrine and Covenants 121–23

Amid intense persecution of the Saints in western Missouri, Joseph Smith wrote a long letter from the Liberty Jail that included Doctrine and Covenants 121, 122, and 123. In some respects the Prophet reached a new degree of greatness as he unfolded the truths of these revelations. "During his incarceration . . . the Prophet Joseph Smith received some of the most rich and remarkable revelations ever given to any prophet. The double walls, four feet thick, kept Joseph and his companions in, but they could not keep the Spirit and revelation out. . . . The . . . prison-temple becomes a unique window itself through which to view Joseph and the process of revelation and soul stretching evident during this particular period of the Restoration" (Maxwell, *Small Moment*, p. 1). The remarkable truths unfolded by the Lord to a Prophet who had been humbled by severe trials are better understood and appreciated as one considers the oppression of the Saints in late 1838 and early 1839, including the experiences which led to the Prophet's being imprisoned at Liberty.

THE SAINTS' SUFFERING

Emily Partridge vividly describes the fall of Far West: "On the morning of the 1st of November, [1838] the bugle sounded for the brethren to assemble. Every man went well armed and was paraded and delivered over to the mob.

"The brethren were surrounded and required to surrender their arms and were guarded all day, while the soldiers went from house to house, plundering, pillaging, destroying and driving, in some instances, women and children from their homes.

"Before the mob disbanded, after securing the arms of the brethren, they rode through the city, and passed so close to our house that we could hear their remarks. . . . I felt no fear, for I had got pretty well used to seeing mobocrats by this time" (*Woman's Exponent*, 1 July 1885, p. 18).

More than fifty Saints were taken prisoners. They were forced to gather in a small circle on the public square and were surrounded by a strong guard. Some, according to Lyman Wight, "were exhibited in a wagon in the town. . . . The aged father and mother of Joseph Smith were not permitted to see his face, but to reach their hands through the curtains of the wagon, and thus take leave of him. When passing his own house, he was taken out of the wagon and permitted to go into the house, but not without a strong guard, and not permitted to speak with his family but in the presence of his guard and his eldest son, Joseph, about six or eight years old, hanging to the tail of his coat, crying father, is the mob going to kill you? The guard said to him, ' . . . You will see your father no more' " (*Times and Seasons*, 15 July 1843, p. 268).

The brethren were forced to march south from Far West. The weather was cold, and when they camped for the night, they lay upon the muddy, wet ground. Some were without a blanket to protect them from the cold and frost.

The Mormon leaders were publicly displayed in the various towns through which they passed. Upon their arrival in Richmond, Parley P. Pratt complained, "Here, as usual, we had to endure the gaze of the curious, as if we had been a caravan of exhibiting animals. We were conducted, with some military parade, into a block house, and immediately put in chains" (*History of Persecution*, p. 25). Most of the leaders were confined in that community for almost one month while they awaited a decision by a court of inquiry, many having been charged with treason.

Parley recalled how one night the guards at the Richmond Jail obscenely boasted of how they had plundered, raped, and murdered the Mormons: "I had listened till I became so disgusted, shocked, horrified, and so filled with the spirit of indignant justice that I could scarcely refrain from rising upon my feet and rebuking the guards; but had said nothing to Joseph, or any one else, although I lay next to him and knew he was awake. On a sudden he arose to his feet, and spoke in a voice of thunder, or as the roaring lion, uttering, as near as I can recollect, the following words:

" '*SILENCE, ye fiends of the infernal pit. In the name of Jesus Christ I rebuke you, and command you to be still; I will not live another minute and bear such language. Cease such talk, or you or I die THIS INSTANT!'*

"He ceased to speak. He stood erect in terrible majesty. Chained, and without a weapon; calm, unruffled and dignified as an angel, he looked upon the quailing guards, whose weapons were lowered or dropped to the ground; whose knees smote together, and who, shrinking into a corner, or crouching at his feet, begged his pardon, and remained quiet till a change of guards" (*Autobiography*, pp. 210–11).

MOVED TO LIBERTY

After weeks of delay, the court found probable cause for charging Joseph Smith and several others with " 'overt acts of treason' in Daviess and Caldwell counties." Four more, including Parley P. Pratt, were charged with murder in Ray County. Since there were not "adequate jail facilities in the counties where the alleged crimes took place," those accused of treason were sent to the Liberty Jail in Clay County, and those accused of murder were retained in the Ray County Jail at Richmond (Jessee, *Personal Writings*, pp. 373–74).

On 1 December 1838, six leaders were transported by wagon to Liberty and placed in a small, twenty-two-foot square jail. Lyman Littlefield, a member of the Church, witnessed the incarceration of the men at that jail: "They were all in one large, heavy wagon with a high box, which, as they were seated, hid from view all of their forms, except from a little below the shoulders. They passed through the center of the town, across the public square, in the center of which stood the court house. After crossing this square the wagon containing them was driven up the street northward about the distance of two blocks, where, at the left hand side of the street, was a vacant piece of ground, upon which, close to the street, stood the Liberty Jail, ever to be rendered famous by the entrance into it of these illustrious prisoners. . . .

"The inhabitants of Liberty, and many from the surrounding country, were out to witness the entrance of the prisoners into the place, and many, on that occasion, in my hearing, expressed their disappointment that the strangers should so much resemble all other men of prepossessing appearance. . . .

"The prisoners left the wagon and immediately ascended the south steps. . . . The door was open, and, one by one, the tall and well proportioned forms of the prisoners entered. The Prophet Joseph was the last of the number who lingered behind. He turned partly around, with a slow and dignified movement, and looked upon the multitude. Then turning away, and, lifting his hat, he said in a distinct voice, 'Good afternoon, gentlemen.' The next moment he had passed out of sight. The heavy door swung upon its strong hinges and the Prophet was hid from the gaze of the curious populace who had so eagerly watched. . . . Finally the excitement subsided, the people dispersed, and the prisoners were left to seek the best rest their hard, dark, and cheerless prison quarters might afford them" (Reminiscences, pp. 79–81).

Liberty Jail was divided into two rooms. A dim light passed through two small windows on the upper floor, and the lower floor was a damp, dark, dreary dungeon. The Prophet was confined in that prison for four months, from 1 December 1838 to 6 April 1839, and during that period approximately ten thousand Latter-day Saints were forced to leave Missouri.

The trials that the Saints experienced during their expulsion from Missouri are vividly reflected in a letter Emma Smith wrote to her husband on 7 March 1839: "I shall not attempt to write my feelings altogether, for the situation in which you are, the walls, bars, and bolts, rolling rivers, running streams, rising hills, sinking vallies and spreading prairies that separate us, and the cruel injustice that first cast you into prison and still holds you there, with many other considerations, places my feelings far beyond description. Was it not for conscious innocence, and the direct interposition of divine mercy, I am very sure I never should have been able to have endured the scenes of suffering that I have passed through, since what is called the Militia, came into Far West, under the ever to be remembered Governor's notable order. . . . No one but God, knows the reflections of my mind and the feelings of my heart when I left our house and home, and allmost all of every thing that we possessed excepting our little children, and took my journey out of the State of Missouri, leaving you shut up in that lonesome prison. But the recollection is more than human nature ought to bear. . . . The daily sufferings of our brethren in travelling and camping out nights, and those on the other side of the river would beggar the most lively description. The people in this state [Illinois] are very kind indeed, they are doing much more than we ever anticipated they would; I have many more things I could like to write but have not time and you may be astonished at my bad writing and incoherent manner, but you will pardon all when you reflect how hard it would be for you to write, when your hands were stiffened with hard work, and your heart convulsed with intense anxiety. But I hope there is better days to come to us yet" (Jessee, *Personal Writings*, pp. 388–89).

EPISTLES FROM LIBERTY JAIL

Shortly after Joseph received his wife's letter, along with letters from two of his brothers and from Bishop Partridge, he responded by " 'writing an epistle to the church.' . . . The lengthy letter produced on March 20 was signed by all the prisoners in the Liberty Jail and contained sentiments that were later published as sections 121–123 of the Doctrine and Covenants. Although this epistle was addressed to the 'church . . . scattered abroad and to Bishop Partridge in particular,' Joseph sent it to his wife with instructions for his family to have the first reading and then convey it to the Church" (Jessee, *Personal Writings*, p. 389).

On 21 March 1839, the day after the Prophet wrote his inspired letter to the Church, he wrote specifically to Emma:

"Affectionate Wife,

"I have sent an Epistle to the church directed to you because I wanted you to have the first reading of it and then I want Father and Mother to have a coppy of it keep the original yourself as I dictated the matter myself and shall send an other as soon as possible I want to be with you very much but the powers of mobocra[c]y is to many for me at present . . . my Dear Emma I very well know your toils and simpathise with you if God will spare my life once more to have the privelege of takeing care of you I will ease your care and indeavour to cumfort your heart [p. 1] I wa[n]t you to take the best care of the family you can which I believe you will do all you can I was sorry to learn that Frederick was sick but I trust he is well again and that you are all well I want you to try to gain time and write to me a long letter and tell me all you can and even if old major [Joseph's dog] is alive yet and what those little pratlers say that cling around you[r] neck do you tell them I am in prison that their lives might be saved I want all the church to make out a bill of damages and apply to the uni = ted states court as soon as possible . . . I blieve that there is a way to git redress for [such] things but God ruleth all things after the council of his own will my trust is in him the salvation of my soul is of the most importants to me . . .

" . . . Dear Emma do you think that my being cast into prison by the mob renders me less worthy of your friends = ship no I do not think so but when I was in prisen and ye viseted me inasmuch as you have don it to the least ⟨of⟩ these you have don[e] it to me these shall enter into life Eternal but no more your Husband J Smith Jr" (Jessee, *Personal Writings*, pp. 408–9). Within a month, Joseph and his companions were able to escape and rejoin the Saints in Illinois.

23

A TEMPLE IN NAUVOO

Doctrine and Covenants 124; 127–28

After escaping from Missouri, the Prophet Joseph Smith established a new place of gathering on a bend in the winding Mississippi River. The name chosen for the new city was *Nauvoo*, a Hebrew word meaning "beautiful." Nearly two years had passed since the revelations recorded in the Doctrine and Covenants as sections 121 through 123 were given at Liberty. The next revelation recorded in the Doctrine Covenants was given at Nauvoo. That communication, as well as other revelations and teachings of the Prophet which unfolded during the last four years of his life, were related to temple worship, covenants, teachings, ordinances, and blessings.

THE DOCTRINE OF BAPTISM FOR THE DEAD IS RESTORED

Although the doctrine of salvation for the dead had been unfolded in Kirtland in 1836 (D&C 137, 110), vicarious ordinances were not performed until four years later at Nauvoo. Joseph Smith first taught the practice of vicarious baptisms for the dead on 15 August 1840 at the funeral of Seymour Brunson, a faithful member of the Nauvoo high council (*History of the Church*, 4:179; see also D&C 124:132). He indicated that the Saints could "now act for their friends who had departed this life, and that the plan of salvation was calculated to save all who were willing to obey the requirements of the law of God" (Ehat, *Words*, p. 49). Soon afterwards, the Saints began receiving this ordinance in the Mississippi River in behalf of deceased loved ones. On a later occasion, Joseph warned: "Those Saints who neglect it in behalf of their deceased relatives, do it at the peril of their own salvation" (*History of the Church*, 4:426).

With such a warning, the Saints eagerly were baptized for their departed loved ones, usually members of their immediate families. In Joseph Smith's own family, for example, Hyrum was baptized for

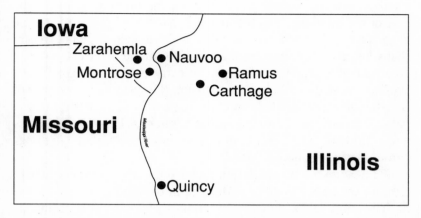

his brother Alvin; Emma received the ordinance for her father, mother, two sisters, an uncle, and an aunt; Lucy was baptized for a sister, her parents, and all four of her grandparents; and Samuel H. Smith was baptized for an uncle (see Cowan, *Temples*, p. 46).

Elder Wilford Woodruff later reflected on the enthusiastic spirit in which these ordinances were first performed: "How did we feel when we first heard the living could be baptized for the dead? We all went to work at it as fast as we had an opportunity, and were baptized for everybody we could think of, without respect to sex. I went and was baptized for all my friends, grandmothers, and aunts, as [well as for] those of the male sex; but how was it? Why, by-and-by, it was revealed, through the servants of the Lord, that females should be baptised for females, and males for males" (*Journal of Discourses*, 5:85).

DIRECTIONS TO BUILD THE TEMPLE

On 19 January 1841, approximately one month after the governor of Illinois signed charters providing guidelines for establishing Nauvoo, Joseph Smith unfolded a revelation (D&C 124) of "monumental importance . . . because its fulfillment engaged nearly every waking moment of the Prophet's time until his death" (Cook, *Revelations*, p. 243). This revelation dealt with the building of Nauvoo in general but gave particular emphasis to the construction of the temple.

The Prophet testified that the basic design for the Nauvoo Temple had been given to him by revelation. For example, when architect William Weeks questioned placing round windows on the side of the building, Joseph explained that "one light at the centre of each circular window would be sufficient to light the whole room; that when the whole building was thus illuminated, the effect would be remarkably grand. 'I wish you to carry out *my* designs,' " the Prophet insisted. " 'I have seen in vision the splendid appearance of that building illuminated, and will have it built according to the pattern shown me' " (*History of the Church,* 6:196–97). This was one fulfillment of the Lord's promise to show the Prophet "all things pertaining to that house" (D&C 124:42).

The January 1841 revelation declared that the ordinance of baptism for the dead should be performed in the Lord's house and that he had temporarily allowed the Saints to perform this ordinance outside the temple (such as in the Mississippi River) only in the days of their poverty. He therefore commanded them to provide an appropriate font in the temple. He would grant them "a sufficient time" to accomplish that, during which period he would continue to accept the baptisms performed in the river (D&C 124:25–32).

The Saints took this revelation seriously, so they hastened the construction of the temple. On 2 October 1841 the Prophet emphatically declared: "There shall be no more baptisms for the dead, until the ordinance can be attended to in the Lord's house; and the Church shall not hold another general Conference, until they can meet in said house. *For thus saith the Lord!"* (*History of the Church,* 4:426). Soon, the temple basement was covered over, and on November 8, Joseph Smith dedicated a temporary wooden font there. On Sunday, November 21, a large congregation gathered in the temple basement to witness the first baptisms for the dead in this new font. Elders Brigham Young, Heber C. Kimball, and John Taylor baptized about forty persons in behalf of their ancestors. Elders Willard Richards, Wilford Woodruff, and George A. Smith performed the confirmation ordinances. Thereafter, the Prophet and members of the Twelve frequently officiated in the temple (*History of the Church,* 4:446–47, 454, 486).

THE SAINTS SACRIFICE TO BUILD A TEMPLE

Constructing an edifice as magnificent as the Nauvoo Temple required considerable sacrifice on the part of the Saints. Because they had little money to give, they willingly donated their labor. Some skilled workmen were hired to work on the temple, sometimes without guarantee of compensation.

Newlywed George Morris was more specific than most journal-keepers in describing how he survived while building the temple: "I received [for working on the temple] flour, cornmeal, bacon, firewood, lumber, brick and now and then a little molasses. I got a little sugar a few times from Charles Allen for digging and tending his garden nights and mornings after working all day on the brickyard. . . . I had money enough left to buy five hundred feet of lumber and I got the privilege to lean a shanty against the house that Brother William Anderson lived in. . . .

"I was not able to get shingles to cover it with so I had to cover it with boards, and the roof being rather flat and the boards being pretty [small]. When it rained it was a little worse than being out of doors. We got along pretty well with that rolling the bed up in as small a compass as we could and putting it in as dry a place as we could find and throwing something over it to keep it dry ("Autobiography," pp. 41–42).

President Brigham Young, speaking at the laying of the cornerstone of the Salt Lake Temple, described the sacrifices of the Nauvoo Saints: "But what of the Temple in Nauvoo? By the aid of sword in one hand, and trowel and hammer in the other, with fire arms at hand, and a strong band of police, and the blessings of heaven, the Saints, through hunger, and thirst, and weariness, and watchings, and prayings, completed the Temple" (*Journal of Discourses*, 2:32).

On a later occasion he again spoke of the Saints' sacrifice: "The last year we staid in Nauvoo, I planted from ten to twelve acres of corn, and I never saw one day, from the time it was planted until it was harvested, in which to spend an hour amongst it. My teams were wanted at the Temple, and, said I, 'Let the corn go.' If they had the teams ready to attend to the corn, the word was, 'Go to the Temple,' and I do not suppose there was a greater crop of corn raised in all Hancock County. I said to the brethren who plowed and planted the land, 'Paul plants and Apollos waters, and if God does not give the increase I can do without it' " (*Journal of Discourses*, 2:271).

The sisters also were involved in building the temple. Sarah M. Kimball's seamstress, Miss Cook, wanted to help, but had no means to contribute. "I told her I would furnish material," Sarah recalled, "if she would make some shirts for the workmen." These sisters realized that others "might wish to combine means and efforts," so they invited some neighbors "to come and consult with us on the subject of forming a Ladies' Society." These discussions resulted in the formation of the Relief Society on 17 March 1842 in Joseph Smith's red brick store (*History of Relief Society*, p. 18). The Relief Society sisters more than met the challenge to contribute one cent per week to purchase nails and glass for the temple.

The Lord directed the Saints to gather precious materials for building the temple (D&C 124:26–27). Louisa Decker recalled how her mother sold their best china dishes and a fine quilt to raise funds (*Woman's Exponent*, Mar. 1909, p. 41). Another example of sacrifice for building the temple was that of Joseph Toronto, a convert from Sicily, who donated his entire life's savings. Brigham Young later remembered: "It was difficult to get bread and other provisions for the workmen to eat. I counseled the committee who had charge of the temple funds to deal out all the flour they had, and God would give them more; and they did so; and it was but a short time before Brother Toronto came and brought me twenty-five hundred dollars in gold . . . so I opened the mouth of the bag and took hold at the bottom end, and gave it a jerk towards the bishop, and strewed the gold across the room and said, now go and buy flour for the workmen on the temple and do not distrust the Lord any more; for we will have what we need" (Roberts, *Comprehensive History*, 2:472).

OTHER ORDINANCES AND
FURTHER INSTRUCTIONS

Joseph Smith continued to receive revelations related to the temple ordinances, including the endowment and celestial marriage, during the construction of the Nauvoo Temple. Although the Saints had received a preliminary or partial endowment in Kirtland, in Nauvoo this ordinance was unfolded more fully. That was accomplished in the large assembly room on the second floor of Joseph Smith's red brick store on 4 May 1842, just seven weeks after the Relief Society was organized.

Joseph Smith recorded: "I spent the day in the upper part of the store . . . in council with [seven brethren], instructing them in the principles and order of the Priesthood, attending to washings, anointings, endowments and the communication of keys pertaining to the Aaronic Priesthood, and so on to the highest order of the Melchisedek Priesthood, setting forth the order pertaining to the Ancient of Days, and all those plans and principles by which any one is enabled to secure the fullness of those blessings which have been prepared for the Church of the First Born, and come up and abide in the presence of the Eloheim in the eternal worlds. . . . The communications I made to this council were of things spiritual, and to be received only by the spiritual minded: and there was nothing made known to these men but what will be made known to all the Saints of the last days, so soon as they are prepared to receive, and a proper place is prepared to communicate them, even to the weakest of the Saints; therefore let the Saints be diligent in building the Temple" (*History of the Church*, 5:1–2). This, in part, fulfilled the Lord's promise to "restore" priesthood ordinances and to reveal "all things" pertaining to his house (D&C 124:28, 42).

The Prophet wrote two letters (D&C 127 and 128) during the first week of September 1842, giving further instructions on work for the dead. At this time, the Prophet was in hiding somewhere in Nauvoo because an attempt had been made on the life of Missouri's Governor Boggs and officials from that state accused Joseph Smith of being involved. In his letters, the Prophet emphasized that there must be "a welding link of some kind or other between the fathers and the children" and that vicarious ordinances for the dead were the means of establishing it (D&C 128:15, 18).

THE SAINTS' EAGERNESS TO
RECEIVE TEMPLE BLESSINGS

After the martyrdom of Joseph and Hyrum Smith on 27 June 1844, the Saints realized they would soon be forced to leave Nauvoo and their temple. Nevertheless, they were willing to sacrifice their time and means to complete the house of the Lord. By the end of November 1845, the attic story was sufficiently completed that it could be dedicated and prepared for giving sacred ordinances. Partitions and furnishings were arranged in the attic story of the temple to represent various stages of man's progress back to the presence of God. When Joseph Fielding first entered the area representing the celestial kingdom, he felt as though he had truly "gotten out of the world" (*BYU Studies*, Winter 1979, pp. 188–89).

Endowments were given beginning December 10. Under the personal leadership of the Twelve, scores of people participated in these blessings each day. Even on Christmas day some 107 individuals received the endowment.

Because of the growing pressure on the Saints to leave Illinois immediately, Church leaders decided to commence the exodus early in February rather than wait until spring. This decision further intensified the Saints' eagerness to receive temple blessings before leaving Nauvoo. On January 12 Brigham Young recorded: "Such has been the anxiety manifested by the saints to receive the ordinances [of the Temple], and such the anxiety on our part to administer to them, that I have given myself up entirely to the work of the Lord in the Temple night and day, not taking more than four hours sleep, upon an average, per day, and going home but once a week" (*History of the Church*, 7:567).

As the time for the exodus drew closer, the pace of work in the temple became even more intense. On February 3 Brigham Young wrote:

"Notwithstanding that I had announced that we would not attend to the administration of the ordinances, the House of the Lord was thronged all day, the anxiety being so great to receive, as if the brethren would have us stay here and continue the endowments until our way would be hedged up, and our enemies would intercept us. But I informed the brethren that this was not wise, and that we should build more Temples, and have further opportunities to receive the blessings of the Lord, as soon as the saints were prepared to receive them. In this Temple we have been abundantly rewarded, if we receive no more. I also informed the brethren that I was going to get my wagons started and be off. I walked some distance from the Temple supposing the crowd would disperse, but on returning I found the house filled to overflowing.

"Looking upon the multitude and knowing their anxiety, as they were thirsting and hungering for the word, we continued at work diligently in the House of the Lord" (*History of the Church*, 7:579).

During the eight weeks before the exodus, approximately fifty-five hundred individuals were endowed. Erastus Snow concluded: "The Spirit, Power, and Wisdom of God reigned continually in the Temple and all felt satisfied that during the two months we occupied it in the endowments of the Saints, we were amply paid for all our labors in building it" (*BYU Studies*, Spring 1979, p. 374).

After many and perhaps most of the Saints had left Nauvoo, the temple was dedicated in a private service on the evening of 30 April 1846. Elder Wilford Woodruff described the service in his journal: "In the evening of this day I repaired to the Temple with Elder Orson Hyde and about twenty other elders of Israel. There we were all clothed in our priestly robes and dedicated the Temple of the Lord. . . . Notwithstanding the predictions of false prophets and the threat of mobs that the building should never be completed nor dedicated, their words had fallen to the ground. The Temple was now finished and dedicated to Him." Elder Hyde repeated the dedicatory prayer in a public service the next day (Cowley, *Woodruff*, pp. 247–48).

Wandle Mace reflected the feelings of the Saints who had been forced to abandon their precious temple: "Farewell to the temple upon which I have labored with so much pleasure, the second temple erected to the only true and living God, in which the ordinances of the Holy Priesthood might be administered to the living and for the dead, in this generation. The order of architecture was unlike anything in existence; it was purely original, being a representation of the Church, the Bride, the Lamb's wife. John, the Revelator in the 12 chapter, first verse says, 'And there appeared a great wonder in heaven; a woman clothed with the sun, and the moon under her feet, and upon her head a crown of twelve stars.' This is portrayed in the beautifully cut stone of this grand temple which cost about two million dollars. The cost was so great, it was said by some that the state of Illinois could not have built such a costly building without bankrupting the state. Yet this was built by the energy, tithes and offerings of an honest, although a poor, persecuted people" ("Autobiography," p. 207).

24

INSTRUCTIONS ON
VARIOUS GOSPEL PRINCIPLES
Doctrine and Covenants 129–32

As doctrinal principles were unfolded to the Prophet Joseph Smith, he gradually taught them to others. Church members learned new truths through personal conversations with the Prophet, listening to him preach, or by reading his letters, revelations, and writings in Church periodicals. Thus, the Nauvoo Saints increased in understanding of the gospel's eternal beauty.

Some distinctive theological teachings of the Prophet are contained in Doctrine and Covenants 129 through 132, which were recorded during 1843 by William Clayton, the Prophet's scribe, and were first included in the 1876 edition of the Doctrine and Covenants.

ITEMS OF INSTRUCTION

The instructions recorded in Doctrine and Covenants 130 and 131 were given by the Prophet during two visits to Ramus, about twenty miles east of Nauvoo, when he went to counsel the Church's substantial branch there. (*Ramus* is a Latin word meaning "branch.") On Sunday, 2 April 1843, during the morning meeting, Orson Hyde, who had come to Ramus with the Prophet, preached on the Last Days. "Alluding to the coming of the Savior, he said, 'When He shall appear, we shall be like Him, &c. He will appear on a white horse as a warrior, and maybe we shall have some of the same spirit. Our God is a warrior (John 14:23). It is our privilege to have the Father and Son dwelling in our hearts, &c.'

"We dined with my sister Sophronia McCleary, when I told Elder Hyde that I was going to offer some corrections to his sermon this morning. He replied, 'They shall be thankfully received' " (*History of the Church*, 5:323). These promised corrections as well as other instructions are now embodied in Doctrine and Covenants 130.

One month later, on 16 and 17 May, the Prophet again taught principles of the gospel to members of the Church at Ramus. On 16 May, Joseph Smith and William Clayton spent the evening with Benjamin F. Johnson and others at the home of William G. Perkins. Before retiring, the Prophet instructed Benjamin F. Johnson on the priesthood. "Putting his hand on the knee of William Clayton, the Prophet said, 'Your life is hid with Christ in God, and so is many others.' Addressing Benjamin F., Joseph said: 'Nothing but the unpardonable sin can prevent him [Clayton] from inheriting eternal glory for he is sealed up by the power of the priesthood unto eternal life having taken the step which is necessary for that purpose' " (*Revelations*, p. 291). Related instructions given during this visit are recorded in Doctrine and Covenants 131.

Benjamin F. Johnson remembered these two visits and the truths unfolded at that time: "On April 2d and May 16th 1843 the Prophet was at my house with Wm Clayton as *scribe* at which time was written in answer to questions asked all of sections 130 & 131 [in the] Doc & Cov and he then gave to us all keys of knowledge contained in sec 129 & 132 of the both before it was written" (Cook, *Revelations*, p. 290).

CELESTIAL MARRIAGE

Eternal marriage was among the blessings unfolded during these years. Although a couple was married for eternity as early as 5 April 1841, there were few of these "sealings" at first. The number of marriages for eternity increased in 1843. In May of that year the Prophet instructed the Saints that to attain the highest degree of the celestial kingdom, they must enter "the new and everlasting covenant of marriage" (D&C 131:1–4). Two months later, on 12 July 1843, Joseph recorded another revelation (D&C 132) in the presence of his brother Hyrum and his private secretary, William Clayton, which declared that only through the power of the priesthood can marriage covenants for eternity be performed. This revelation also confirmed the principle, revealed as early as 1831, that authorized worthy men to marry more wives than one (D&C 132:34–65).

According to Joseph F. Smith, "Joseph Smith was commanded to take wives, he hesitated and postponed it, seeing the consequences and the trouble that it would bring and he shrank from the responsibility, but he prayed to the Lord for it to pass as Jesus did, but . . . the Lord had revealed it to him, and said now is the time for it to be practised but it was not untill he had been told he must practice it or be destroyed that he made the attempt—in 1841 he had wives sealed to him—from that time untill his death he had wives sealed unto him. Emma, his wife yielded but it was not without considerable argument that she consented and with her own hand gave to Joseph Smith four wives in this new and everlasting covenant their names are Emily and Eliza Partridge and Sarah and Maria Lawrence the latter two being sisters. . . . Soon after the marriage of Joseph to the four ladies mentioned Emma repented of having given them to Joseph and told Joseph that if [he] would not give them up, she would bring him up before the law and became very bitter about this time under this threat and on account of the determined manner of Emma, Joseph went to his brother Hyrum and had a talk with him about it. Hyrum told Joseph if you will write the Revelation [D&C 132] I will take it and go and see Emma for I can convince her that it is true. Joseph smiled at Hyrum saying you do not know Emma as well as I do—but Hyrum said he still had faith that he could do as he said, and to satisfy his brother Hyrum, Joseph caused the Revelation to be written on the 12th July 1843. Joseph with Hyrum went into the office and Joseph commanded Wm. Clayton to write as he should dictate. Joseph was asked by Hyrum to get the Urim and Thummim. Joseph said he knew it from beginning to end, he then dictated it word for word to Wm. Clayton as it is now in the Doctrine and Covenants it was written for this purpose at Hyrums suggestion, after it was done, Joseph said there that is enough for the present, but I have a great deal more, which would be given hereafter; Hyrum went to Emma and returned without making any impression upon her" (Cook, *Revelations*, pp. 347–48).

Learning that William Clayton had written the revelation as it was dictated by the Prophet, Edward Stevenson commented: "By this revelation, not only a flood of light followed, but bitter persecution as well. Those principles had been lost to the human families for centuries and now in the midst of tradition, it cost precious blood to establish them again. In a public discourse 16 July 1843, Joseph said to some sitting on the stand when he was preaching and he placed his hand on one or two saying, 'If I were to reveal the things God has made known unto me, my life would be sought in the streets of Nauvoo' " ("Autobiography," p. 94).

Warren Foote was one of many Saints who recorded his response to various distinguishing doctrines that were unfolded by the Prophet during the Nauvoo years: "We went to see Brother Duncan Mc-Arthur, with whom we were well acquainted. Having learned that he was one of the number who had been appointed to teach the principle of Celestial Marriage to the Saints, according to the revelation [D&C 132] given to Joseph Smith on that subject, we desired to get some correct information on that principle. The doctrine having never been taught publicly, there were all sorts of reports concerning it. He very willingly taught and explained to us that doctrine in such a simple manner. . . . He showed us the necessity of marriage for eternity in order to obtain an exaltation in the Celestial Kingdom. I felt to rejoice, that the doubts and fears that had been resting on my mind with regard to plural marriage caused by the traditions of the Fathers, were all removed. By the aid of the light of the Spirit, I could in a measure see the glory and beauty of that principle. It was very plain that our marriage covenants were only for time, they last only through this life. We are not bound as husbands and wives for eternity but all our domestic relations were dissolved at death. We learned that the celestial law binds for time and eternity, and our connection as husbands and wives, parents, and children never ceases in time nor all eternity, and we will continue to increase while eternities roll around" ("Autobiography," p. 64).

During the winter of 1839–40, Joseph met Parley P. Pratt and taught him for the first time the doctrine of celestial marriage. As Elder Pratt considered that glorious principle, he gained a new understanding of other principles of the gospel, including man's relationship to God, characteristics of the Godhead, plurality of gods, and premortal life. He further recognized that there was a harmony among these teachings and, being acquainted with various religious systems, understood that these concepts were distinct theological contributions of Joseph Smith. Recalling this sudden expansion of knowledge, he wrote:

"It was from him that I learned that the wife of my bosom might be secured to me for time and all eternity; and that the refined sympathies and affections which endeared us to each other emanated from the fountain of divine eternal love. It was from him that I learned that we might cultivate these affections, and grow and increase in the same to all eternity; while the result of our endless union would be an offspring as numerous as the stars of heaven, or the sands of the sea shore.

"It was from him that I learned the true dignity and destiny of a son of God, clothed with an eternal priesthood, as the patriarch and sovereign of his countless offspring. It was from him that I learned that the highest dignity of womanhood was, to stand as a queen and priestess to her husband, and to reign for ever and ever as the queen mother of her numerous and still increasing offspring. . . .

" . . . I felt that God was my heavenly Father indeed; that Jesus was my brother, and that the wife of my bosom was an immortal, eternal companion; a kind ministering angel, given to me as a comfort, and a crown of glory for ever and ever. In short, I could now love with the spirit and with the understanding also.

"Yet, at that time, my dearly beloved brother, Joseph Smith, had barely touched a single key; [he] had merely lifted a corner of the veil and given me a single glance into eternity" (*Autobiography*, pp. 297–98).

25

CONTRIBUTIONS OF A LATTER-DAY PROPHET

Doctrine and Covenants 135

All the revelations studied thus far were given through the Prophet Joseph Smith. His brutal murder in the Carthage Jail on 27 June 1844 led many to predict the imminent demise of the work he had founded. That, of course, did not come to pass. Still, that tragic event provided the occasion to assess the significance of Joseph Smith's role as prophet of the Restoration.

THE MARTYRDOM

Events leading to the Martyrdom began when the Nauvoo city council ordered that the slanderous, anti-Mormon newspaper, the *Nauvoo Expositor*, be closed down because it was a "nuisance." Joseph Smith was targeted by his enemies because as mayor he had signed the order to destroy the press, and they immediately began plotting ways to take his life. Believing that the mob wanted only him, Joseph decided to spare the Saints by crossing the Mississippi River and heading an expedition to the West. Joseph remarked to a close associate, "If I and Hyrum were ever taken again we should be massacred, or I was not a prophet of God." After learning that some in Nauvoo believed he was cowardly for running away, the Prophet said, "If my life is of no value to my friends it is of none to myself" (*History of the Church*, 6:546, 549). He returned to Nauvoo, where he surrendered to the militia, which escorted him to Carthage for trial, going "like a lamb to the slaughter" (D&C 135:4). Joseph Smith was held illegally in the Carthage Jail on a trumped-up charge of treason, which provided his enemies an opportunity to murder the Mormon leader.

Benjamin Ashby's recollections captured the feelings of the Saints at that critical time in Church history: "I was in my father's garden one morning . . . when he [Joseph Smith] rode past on his way to Carthage. Never shall I forget the look of deep sorrow that covered his noble countenance—that was the last time I saw him alive. . . . I sat upon the steps of my father's house on the evening of the day that he was shot until twelve o'clock and never did I hear before such an uproar and noise that seemed to pervade the very atmosphere; dogs howling, mingled with confused noises as though all the legions of the damned were in commotion.

"Not dreaming of the tragedy that had been enacted that afternoon, I went to bed but at the dawn of morning the sad tale was brought to our ears and the grief and sorrow of a whole people cannot be pictured in language; for days, a man, woman or child could not be met but they were in tears for the loss of their beloved leader. Soon the wagons containing the two brothers arrived in the city and passed down to the Mansion House where we visited and viewed their marred features as they lay in the hallowments of the grave" ("Autobiography," pp. 9–10).

Parley P. Pratt, who was on a mission in the East at the time of the Martyrdom, described his feelings on that occasion: "A day or two previous to this circumstance I had been constrained by the Spirit to start prematurely for home, without knowing why or wherefore; and on the same afternoon I was passing on a canal boat near Utica, New York, on my way to Nauvoo. My brother, William Pratt, being then on a mission in the same state (New York), happened, providentially, to take passage on the same boat. As we conversed together on the deck, a strange and solemn awe came over me, as if the powers of hell were let loose. I was so overwhelmed with sorrow I could hardly speak; and after pacing the deck for some time in silence, I turned to my brother William and exclaimed—'Brother William, this is a dark hour; the powers of darkness seem to triumph, and the spirit of murder is abroad in the land; and it controls the hearts of the American people, and a vast majority of them sanction the killing of the innocent. My brother, let us keep silence and not open our mouths. If you have any pamphlets or books on the fulness of the gospel lock them up; show them not, neither open your mouth to the people; let us observe an entire and solemn silence, for this is a dark day, and the hour of triumph for the powers of darkness. O, how sensible I am of the spirit of murder which seems to pervade the whole land.' This was June 27, 1844, in the afternoon, and as near as I can judge, it was the same hour that the Carthage mob were shedding the blood of Joseph and Hyrum Smith, and John Taylor, near one thousand miles distant. . . .

"The steamer touched at a landing in Wisconsin, some fifty or sixty miles from Chicago, and here some new passengers came on board and brought the news of the martyrdom of Joseph and Hyrum Smith. Great excitement prevailed on board, there being a general spirit of exultation and triumph at this glorious news, as it was called. . . .

"Many passengers now gathered about me and tauntingly inquired what the Mormons would do now, seeing their Prophet and leader was killed.

"To these taunts and questions I replied, that they would continue their mission and spread the work he had restored, in all the world. Observing that nearly all the prophets and Apostles who were before him had been killed, and also the Saviour of the world, and yet their death did not alter the truth nor hinder its final triumph" (Autobiography, pp. 331–32).

THE LAW OF WITNESSES FULFILLED

An uncommon characteristic of the Restoration was an emphasis on witnesses, consistent with biblical teachings in 2 Corinthians 13:1. Unlike other religious leaders, Joseph Smith surrounded himself with an array of witnesses who substantiated many of his religious experiences.

As far as we know, when the priesthood and various keys of the priesthood were restored to the earth, another witness was always present and received the same powers conferred upon Joseph. Oliver Cowdery was present during the restoration of the lesser and the higher priesthoods. He was also present and received along with Joseph Smith the keys restored by Moses, Elias, and Elijah (Joseph Smith–History 1:72; and note on pp. 57–58; D&C 13; 110). Thus, Joseph Smith and Oliver Cowdery were the two witnesses of the restoration of priesthood authority.

At the time of the Martyrdom, Hyrum Smith not only was the Patriarch of the Church but also occupied the unique office of Associate President. He had been called to this office three years earlier to stand as a witness in the place of Oliver Cowdery, who had apostatized (D&C 124:91–96). Hence, the two who died at Carthage were the two witnesses of the Restoration who sealed their testimony through the shedding of their blood (D&C 135:5; Hebrews 9:16–17).

UNCOMMON CONTRIBUTIONS OF JOSEPH SMITH

After the Martyrdom, John Taylor wrote a tribute to the Prophet in which he emphasized that Joseph Smith had sealed his testimony with his blood and had done more for the salvation of mankind than any other person, save Jesus Christ (D&C 135:3). Joseph Smith's contributions are not only distinct from those of any other mortal but also from any other prophet. He headed the dispensation of the fullness of times, in which all truths from former ages were restored to the earth. Unlike most "restorationists" of the early nineteenth century, who sought to emulate a pattern of belief and worship described in the New Testament, Joseph Smith taught that the restoration which he directed was much more, that it was in fact a restitution of all things spoken by the mouth of all of God's prophets since the world began. Joseph Smith explained that the prophecy in Acts 3:21 had been fulfilled with a restoration by means of heavenly messengers and modern revelation of all doctrines, covenants, ordinances, blessings, authority, and power unfolded and held by all ancient prophets from the time of Adam to the days of Peter, James, and John (Ehat, *Words*, pp. 10, 39, 43–44, 246).

The Prophet brought forth many historical and doctrinal truths that were not found in the Old and New Testaments. That information is found in Joseph Smith's Inspired Revision or "New Translation" of the Bible, as well as in other latter-day scriptures.

One unusual record brought forth by the Prophet Joseph Smith was the Book of Mormon. This work, unlike any other book, declares that it was written by ancient American prophets for a later generation. It also contains an unusually powerful description of the gospel of Jesus Christ as embraced by those early Americans.

A second book brought forth by Joseph Smith was the Doctrine and Covenants. Building upon the foundation of the Book of Mormon, this book of latter-day scripture contains scores of revelations that unfold, in even more detail, the basic principles, ordinances, and practices of the gospel.

John Taylor affirmed in April 1878 that one of the greatest contributions of Joseph Smith was his inauguration of the dispensation of the fullness of times, "a dispensation in which all other dispensations are merged or concentrated. It embraces and embodies all the other dispensations that have existed upon the earth wherein God communicated himself to the human family" (*Journal of Discourses*, 21:94). After John the Baptist and Peter, James, and John had restored the Aaronic and the Melchizedek priesthoods to Joseph Smith and Oliver Cowdery, "Adam, Noah, Abraham, Moses, Elijah, Elias, and many other leading characters mentioned in the Scriptures, who had operated in the various dispensations, came and conferred upon Joseph the various keys, powers, rights, privileges, and immunities which they enjoyed in their times." President Taylor further emphasized that the knowledge, intelligence, priesthood, powers, and revelations which had been conferred upon various prophets in different ages were "restored to the earth by the ministration and through the medium of those who held the holy Priesthood of God in the different dispensations in which they lived" (*Journal of Discourses*, 23:48–49).

Many aspects of Mormon history cannot be understood without recognizing the unusual belief of Latter-day Saints regarding Joseph Smith's distinct contributions. While members of this religious community experienced greater persecution than adherents of any other Christian church in the young American republic, their faith in the Restoration was the motivating power that enabled them to endure the refiner's fire and cross and tame a vast desert. Their faith was also the dominant force propelling self-supporting missionaries to serve throughout the world. Moreover, it was the power that motivated converts to participate in one of the unusual episodes in world history, the worldwide gathering of a religious community. Like a few other groups, Latter-day Saints gathered to seek refuge, to learn doctrines, to be purified and to prepare for the Second Coming. But unlike others, they gathered to receive blessings in sacred temples. The Latter-day Saints believe that these and other blessings were restored by the Prophet Joseph Smith during the dispensation when there truly has been a restitution of all things.

26

REVELATION CONTINUES

Doctrine and Covenants 136; 138;
Official Declarations 1–2

Enemies of the Saints were confident that with the death of
Joseph Smith, "Mormonism," as they termed it, would quickly col-
lapse. That, however, was not to be the case.

BRIGHAM YOUNG: SUCCESSOR TO JOSEPH SMITH

As the shock of the Martyrdom wore off, the Saints wondered
who could take the place of "brother Joseph" as their prophet-leader.
As early as 1832, on the very day that Joseph Smith first met Brigham
Young, the Prophet had said, "the time will come when brother
Brigham Young will preside over this Church" (*Millennial Star*, 11
July 1863, p. 439).

In 1841, the Lord had urged the construction of the temple so
that he might restore "the fullness of the priesthood" (D&C 124:28).
During the closing year of his life, the Prophet Joseph Smith made
sure that the Twelve and others received the highest blessings available through temple ordinances so that the authority necessary to
roll forth the Lord's work would remain on the earth. Elder Orson
Hyde later recalled that Joseph Smith "conducted us through every
ordinance of the holy priesthood, and when he had gone through
with all the ordinances he rejoiced very much, and says, now if they
kill me you have got all the keys, and all the ordinances and you
can confer them upon others, and the hosts of Satan will not be able
to tear down the kingdom" (*Times and Seasons*, 15 Sept. 1844, p.
651).

Nearly a half century later, President Wilford Woodruff recalled
the Prophet's instructions: "He stood upon his feet some three hours.
The room was filled as with consuming fire, his face was as clear
as amber, and he was clothed upon by the power of God. He laid
before us our duty. He laid before us the fullness of this great work

of God; and in his remarks to us he said: 'I have had sealed upon my head every key, every power, every principle of life and salvation that God has ever given to any man who ever lived upon the face of the earth. . . . 'Now,' said he addressing the Twelve, 'I have sealed upon your heads every key, every power, and every principle which the Lord has sealed upon my head. . . .

" ' . . . I tell you, the burden of this kingdom now rests upon your shoulders; you have got to bear it off in all the world, and if you don't do it you will be damned' " (*Deseret News Weekly*, 19 Mar. 1892, p. 406).

After the martyrdom of Joseph Smith, the apostles who were serving missions returned to Nauvoo. On 7 August 1844, the morning after Brigham Young returned, he and other apostles met at the home of John Taylor, who was recovering from wounds he had received in the Carthage Jail. They discussed the claims of Sidney Rigdon, who contended that he should replace Joseph Smith as "guardian" of the Church. The apostles then called a meeting that afternoon for all high priests. During that meeting Brigham Young said, "I have the keys and the means of obtaining the mind of God on the subject [of succession to the presidency]. . . . Joseph conferred upon our heads [the Twelve] all the keys and powers belonging to the Apostleship which he himself held before he was taken away" (*History of the Church*, 7:230).

The following day, 8 August, the Saints gathered at ten in the morning at a special meeting called by William Marks, president of the Nauvoo Stake. It was a cold, rainy day. Because the wind was blowing towards the stand from where the Saints had gathered, Rigdon left the stand and climbed on a wagon behind the congregation so that they could better hear his voice. The crowd of about five thousand turned around on their benches and faced the wagon. After Rigdon spoke for about one and a half hours, presenting his claim to the presidency, Brigham Young spoke briefly, comforting the Saints. During his speech, many Saints testified, they beheld a miracle. Benjamin Johnson recalled that "President Brigham Young arose and spoke. I saw him arise, but as soon as he spoke I jumped upon my feet, for in every possible degree it was Joseph's voice, and his person, in look, attitude, dress and appearance was Joseph himself, personified; and I knew in a moment the spirit and mantle of Joseph was upon him" (Benjamin Johnson, *My Life's Review*, pp. 103–4).

Helen Mar Whitney said that she could bear witness "with

hundreds of others who stood that day under the sound of Brigham's voice, of the wonderful and startling effect that it had upon us. If Joseph had risen from the dead and stood before them, it could hardly have made a deeper or more lasting impression. It was the very voice of Joseph himself. This was repeatedly spoken of by the Latter-day Saints. And surely it was a most powerful and convincing testimony to them that he was the man, instead of Sidney Rigdon, that was destined to become the 'great leader,' and upon whose shoulders the mantle of Joseph had fallen" (*Woman's Exponent*, 1 Feb. 1883, p. 130).

SUCCESSION IN THE PRESIDENCY
AND CONTINUING REVELATION

Thus it was Brigham Young, at the head of the Quorum of the Twelve Apostles, who led the Saints in their epic trek to the Rocky Mountains. Doctrine and Covenants 136 was given through him to organize the pioneers and instruct them how to deal with each other.

In 1847, after Brigham Young had led the Saints to Utah and returned to Winter Quarters, he selected two counselors, and a First Presidency once again presided over the Church. Upon President Young's death in 1877, John Taylor, at the time president of the Twelve, succeeded him as president of the Church. Similarly, Wilford Woodruff became the fourth president of the Church upon the death of President John Taylor. Wilford Woodruff was thus the prophet and president of the Church in 1890 when he was inspired to write the Manifesto (Official Declaration 1), announcing that the contracting of plural marriages was to be discontinued. The fifth prophet, Lorenzo Snow, was similarly inspired as he called on the Saints to be more faithful in paying their tithing. Near the end of his life, Joseph F. Smith, the sixth prophet, received the remarkable vision of the Savior's ministry in the spirit world that is recorded in Doctrine and Covenants 138.

REVELATION TO AN EXPANDING CHURCH

The Church of Jesus Christ of Latter-day Saints entered a period of unprecedented growth in the second half of the twentieth century (see Richard O. Cowan, *The Church in the Twentieth Century*, chapters 14 and 21). This expansion brought the Church into contact with an increasing number of ethnic groups and cultures worldwide. For example, beginning in 1975 Church members of African descent were actively involved in fund-raising and other activities connected with constructing the temple in Sao Paulo, Brazil. Helvecio Martins, a member of the Church and a respected black business executive and educator from Rio de Janeiro, was appointed to coordinate public relations for the temple project. On one occasion he recounts, "I went onto the Temple construction with my wife, walking among the construction metals and wood and stopped at a certain place. We felt an unusually strong spirit at that time. We held each other and cried for some time. We realized later we were standing at the exact spot of the Celestial Room of the Temple. We felt a strong undescribable feeling in that place. Impressive! Extraordinarily strong. It was one of the most spiritual experiences of our lives" (Martins, interview, p. 16). When President Spencer W. Kimball was in Sao Paulo for the temple cornerstone laying in March 1977, he saw Brother Martins in the audience and asked him to come to the stand briefly. The President said, "Brother, what is necessary for you is faithfulness. Remain faithful and you will enjoy all the blessings of the Church" (p. 23). Martins returned to his seat wondering what the prophet meant (pp. 16, 23).

During this time, Church leaders pondered the policy according to which blacks were not permitted priesthood ordination. President Kimball recalled: "I went to the temple alone, and especially on Sundays and Saturdays when there were not organizations in the temple, when I could have it alone. It went on for some time as I was searching for this, because I wanted to be sure. We held a meeting of the Council of the Twelve in the temple on the regular day [1 June 1978]. We considered this very seriously and thoughtfully and prayerfully.

"I asked the Twelve not to go home when the time came. I said, 'Now would you be willing to remain in the temple with us?' And they were. I offered the final prayer and I told the Lord if it wasn't right, if He didn't want this change to come in the Church that I would be true to it all the rest of my life and I'd fight the world against it if that's what He wanted.

"We had this special prayer circle, then I knew that the time had come. I had a great deal to fight, of course, myself largely, because I had grown up with this thought that Negroes should not have the priesthood and I was prepared to go all the rest of my life till my death and fight for it and defend it as it was. But this revelation and assurance came to me so clearly that there was no question about it" (*Church News*, 6 Jan. 1979, p. 4).

Elder Bruce R. McConkie wrote of this sacred occasion: "It was during this prayer that the revelation came. The Spirit of the Lord rested mightily upon us all; we felt something akin to what happened on the day of Pentecost and at the dedication of the Kirtland Temple. From the midst of eternity, the voice of God, conveyed by the power of the Spirit, spoke to his prophet. The message was that the time had now come to offer the fulness of the everlasting gospel, including celestial marriage, and the priesthood, and the blessings of the temple, to all men, without reference to race or color, solely on the basis of personal worthiness. And we all heard the same voice, received the same message, and became personal witnesses that the word received was the mind and will and voice of the Lord. . . .

"In the days that followed the receipt of the new revelation, President Kimball and President Ezra Taft Benson—the senior and most spiritually experienced ones among us—both said, expressing the feelings of us all, that neither of them had ever experienced anything of such spiritual magnitude and power as was poured out upon the Presidency and the Twelve that day in the upper room in the house of the Lord" (*Priesthood*, p. 128).

One week later, 8 June 1978, the First Presidency approved the official announcement of this revelation (Official Declaration 2). The Sao Paulo Temple was dedicated in October that same year. President Kimball was gratified to see Brother and Sister Martins there: "I don't know when I have ever been as touched as I was to see that man and his wife in the congregation when we were dedicating the Sao Paulo Temple, and to see them wipe their eyes all through the session. They were so thrilled to be permitted to have the blessings" (*Church News*, 6 Jan. 1979, p. 4). On 31 March 1990 Helvecio Martins was sustained as a member of the Quorums of the Seventy, becoming the Church's first black General Authority.

Many people believe that revelation ceased with the publication of the Bible. Nevertheless, insisted President Kimball, we do not accept the idea "that the Old Testament constituted the total words of God's prophets; nor do we believe the New Testament to be the end of revelation. We testify that rather than an end of revelations of God, they continue to pour forth from God for the welfare and benefit of men." After the time of the Savior and his apostles, there were centuries of spriritual darkness known as the great apostasy.

But, continued President Kimball, "I bear witness to the world today that more than a century and a half ago the iron ceiling was shattered; the heavens were once again opened, and since that time revelations have been continuous." The young man Joseph Smith "broke the spell, shattered the 'heavens of iron' and reestablished communication. . . . A new prophet was in the land and through him God set up his kingdom, never to be destroyed nor left to another people — a kingdom that will stand forever. . . .

"Since that momentous day in 1820, additional scripture has continued to come, including the numerous and vital revelations flowing in a never-ending stream from God to his prophets on the earth. Many of these revelations are recorded in another scripture called the Doctrine and Covenants. . . .

"There are those who would assume that with the printing and binding of these sacred records, that would be the 'end of the prophets.' But again we testify to the world that revelation continues and that the vaults and files of the Church contain these revelations which come month to month and day to day. We testify also that there is, since 1830 when The Church of Jesus Christ of Latter-day Saints was organized, and will continue to be, so long as time shall last, a prophet, recognized of God and his people, who will continue to interpret the mind and will of the Lord" (*Ensign*, May 1977, pp. 76–78).

BIBLIOGRAPHY

BOOKS AND PAMPHLETS

Backman, Milton V., Jr. *The Heavens Resound*. Salt Lake City: Deseret Book Co., 1983.

Backman, Milton V., Jr., and Lyndon W. Cook, eds. *Kirtland Elders' Quorum Record*. Provo, Utah: Grandin Book Co., 1985.

Cannon, Donald Q., and Lyndon W. Cook, eds. *Far West Record: Minutes of the Church of Jesus Christ of Latter-day Saints, 1830–1844*. Salt Lake City: Deseret Book Co., 1983.

Classic Experiences and Adventures. Salt Lake City: Bookcraft, 1969.

Cook, Lyndon W., ed. *Revelations of the Prophet Joseph Smith*. Salt Lake City: Deseret Book Co., 1985.

Cowan, Richard O. *The Church in the Twentieth Century*. Salt Lake City: Bookcraft, 1985.

———. *Temples to Dot the Earth*. Salt Lake City: Bookcraft, 1989.

Cowley, Matthias F. *Wilford Woodruff: History of His Life and Labors As Recorded in His Daily Journals*. Salt Lake City: Bookcraft, 1964.

Ehat, Andrew F., and Lyndon W. Cook, eds. *The Words of Joseph Smith*. Provo, Utah: Religious Studies Center, Brigham Young University, 1980.

Four Faith Promoting Classics. Salt Lake City: Bookcraft, 1968.

History of Relief Society, 1842–1966. Salt Lake City: Relief Society General Board, 1966.

Jessee, Dean C., comp. and ed. *The Personal Writings of Joseph Smith*. Salt Lake City: Deseret Book Co., 1984.

Johnson, Benjamin F. *My Life's Review*. Independence, Mo.: Zion's Printing and Publishing Co., 1947.

Johnson, Joel. *Voice from the Mountains, Being a Testimony of the Truth of the Gospel of Jesus Christ, As Revealed by the Lord to Joseph Smith, Jr*. Salt Lake City: Juvenile Instructor, 1881.

Journal of Discourses. Liverpool, England: Latter-day Saints Book Depot, 1886.

Littlefield, Lyman Omer. *Reminiscences of Latter-day Saints*. Logan, Utah: Utah Journal Co., 1888.

Maxwell, Neal A. *But for a Small Moment*. Salt Lake City: Bookcraft, 1986.

Pratt, Orson. *Orson Pratt Journals.* Edited by Elden J. Watson. Salt Lake City: Watson, *Priesthood.* Salt Lake City: Deseret Book Co., 1981.

Pratt, Parley P. *Autobiography of Parley P. Pratt.* Edited by Parley P. Pratt, Jr. Salt Lake City: Deseret Book Co., 1966.

——. *History of the Late Persecution Inflicted by the State of Missouri upon the Mormons.* Detroit, Mich.: Dawson and Bates, 1839.

Priesthood. Salt Lake City: Deseret Book Co., 1981.

Roberts, Brigham H. *A Comprehensive History of the Church of Jesus Christ of Latter-day Saints.* 6 vols. Provo, Utah: Brigham Young University Press, 1965.

Smith, Joseph. *History of the Church of Jesus Christ of Latter-day Saints.* 7 vols. 2d ed. rev. Salt Lake City: Deseret Book Co., 1959.

Smith, Lucy Mack. *History of the Prophet Joseph Smith.* Edited by Preston Nibley. Salt Lake City: Bookcraft, 1958.

Smith, William. *On Mormonism.* Lamoni, Iowa: Herald Steam Book and Job Office, 1883.

Snow, Eliza R. *Biography and Family Record of Lorenzo Snow.* Salt Lake City: Deseret News, 1884.

Stevenson, Edward. *Reminiscences of Joseph, the Prophet, and the Coming Forth of the Book of Mormon.* Salt Lake City: Edward Stevenson, 1893.

Tullidge, Edward W. *The Women of Mormondom.* New York: Tullidge & Crandall, 1877.

Whitmer, David. *Address to All Believers in Christ.* Richmond, Mo.: David Whitmer, 1887.

Whitmer, John. *An Early Latter-day Saint History: The Book of John Whitmer.* Edited by F. Mark McKiernan and Roger D. Launius. Independence, Mo.: Herald Publishing House, 1980.

PERIODICALS

Autumn Leaves. Lamoni, Iowa, 1888–1928.

Brigham Young University Studies. Provo, Utah, 1959–.

Church News (weekly supplement to the *Deseret News*). Salt Lake City, 1931–.

Deseret News. Salt Lake City, 1850–.

Ensign. Salt Lake City, 1971–.

Ensign of Liberty of the Church of Christ. Kirtland, Ohio, 1849.

Improvement Era. Salt Lake City, 1897–1970.

Juvenile Instructor. Salt Lake City, 1866–1970.

Messenger and Advocate. Kirtland, Ohio, 1834–1837.

Millennial Star. Manchester and Liverpool, England, 1840–1970.

The Return. Davis City, Iowa, 1889–1900.

Saints Herald. Independence, Missouri, 1860–.

Utah Genealogical and Historical Magazine. Salt Lake City, 1910–40.

Woman's Exponent. Salt Lake City, 1872–1914.

THESES

Gunnell, Wayne. "Martin Harris." Master's thesis, Brigham Young University, 1955.

Woodford, Robert J. "The Historical Development of the Doctrine and Covenants." Doctoral dissertation, Brigham Young University, 1974.

INTERVIEW

Martins, Helvecio. Interview in Portuguese, 1982. Harold B. Lee Library, Brigham Young University, Provo, Utah.

MANUSCRIPT SOURCES

The following manuscripts (except the Kirtland Council Minute Book) are all taken from a computerized database compiled by Milton V. Backman, Jr., entitled "Writings of Early Latter-day Saints and Their Contemporaries," which is available in the Harold B. Lee Library at Brigham Young University. Spelling, punctuation, and grammar have been standardized.

Ashby, Benjamin. "Autobiography" (1828–46). Copy of holograph. Special Collections, Brigham Young University, Provo, Utah.

Baldwin, Nathan. "Autobiography." Typescript. LDS Church Archives, Salt Lake City.

Carter, Jared. "Autobiography" (1831–33). LDS Church Archives, Salt Lake City.

Crosby, Jonathan. "Autobiography," (1807–52). Typescript and holograph. Utah State Historical Society, Salt Lake City.

Foote, Warren. "Autobiography" (1817–46). Typescript. Special Collections, Brigham Young University, Provo, Utah.

Hancock, Levi Ward. "Autobiography," (1803–36). Typescript. Special Collections.

Hancock, Mosiah. "Autobiography" (1834–75). Typescript. Special Collections, Brigham Young University, Provo, Utah.

Johnson, Joel Hills. "Autobiography" (1802–68). Typescript. Special Collections, Brigham Young University, Provo, Utah.

Kirtland Council Minute Book. Manuscript. LDS Church Archives, Salt Lake City.

Lyman, Eliza Marie Partridge Smith. "Autobiography" (1820–46). Typescript. Special Collections, Brigham Young University, Provo, Utah.

Mace, Wandle. "Autobiography" (1809–46). Typescript. Special Collections, Brigham Young University, Provo, Utah.

Morris, George. "Autobiography" (1816–48). Typescript. Special Collections, Brigham Young University, Provo, Utah.

Pulsipher, Zera. "Autobiography" (c. 1803–39). Typescript. Special Collections, Brigham Young University, Provo, Utah.

Rigdon, John Wickliff. "Life Story of Sidney Rigdon." Holograph. LDS Church Archives, Salt Lake City.

Salt Lake School of Prophets. Minutes, 1883.

Stevenson, Edward. "Autobiography of Edward Stevenson" (1820–46).

Tanner, Elizabeth. "Autobiography of Elizabeth Beswick Tanner." Typescript. Special Collections, Brigham Young University, Provo, Utah.

Tracy, Nancy Naomi Alexander. "Autobiography" (1816–46). Typescript. Special Collections, Brigham Young University, Provo, Utah.

Wight, Orange L. "Autobiography" (1823–1903). Typescript. Special Collections, Brigham Young University, Provo, Utah.

Winters, Mary. "Autobiography" (1833–52). Typescript. LDS Church Archives, Salt Lake City.

Young, Emily Dow Partridge Smith. "Autobiography" (1824–33). Typescript. Brigham Young University Archives, Provo, Utah.

SCRIPTURE INDEX

SUBJECT INDEX

Aaronic priesthood restored, 19
Adam-ondi-Ahman, 111; Prophet
    identifies, 114–15
Alcohol, use of, banned, 83
Allen, Charles, 89–90, 131
Allen, Felatiah, 66
Anderson, William, 131
Angell, Truman O., 86
Apostles, Twelve, vision of the, 105–6
Appendix to Book of Commandments,
    3
Articles and Covenants approved at
    conference, 27
Ashby, Benjamin, 141–42

Baldwin, Nathan, 99
Baptism for the dead, 128–29; to be
    performed in temple, 130
Benson, Ezra Taft, 150
Bible, New Translation of the: Rigdon
    called as scribe for, 44
Black Pete, 57
Blacks, policy regarding, 149
Blake, Captain, 50
Boggs, Lilburn W., 62
Book of Commandments, 1–2. *See also*
    Doctrine and Covenants. Preface to
    the, 2; rescue of, 3, 90; appendix to
    the, 3; revelations added to, 27
Book of Mormon: witnesses to the, 22–
    24; publication of, 24–25;
    opposition to publication of, 24–25
Booth, Ezra, 63
Boynton, John F., 118
Brunson, Seymour, 128
Buffalo, Mormons escape from, 51

Campbell, Alexander, 43
Carter, Jared, 70–71
Carter, Simeon, 38

Catteraugus Indians, 40
Celestial Kingdom, vision of the, 104
Celestial marriage, 132, 137
Cheney, Elijah, 72
Cholera strikes Zion's Camp, 101
Church: organization of the, 25–27;
    first conference of the, 27, 29–30;
    official name of the, 113; period of
    growth of, 148
"Church of Christ," 112
Church of the Latter-day Saints, 112
Civil War, American, 75–76
Clay County, Saints settle in, 93
Clayton, William, 136–37
Colesville Saints, 47–28; travel to
    Missouri, 59–60
Coltrin, Zebedee, speaks in tongues,
    77; on the School of the Prophets,
    78–80; on the Word of Wisdom, 81;
    vision of, 106
"Common stock," 53–54
Consecration, law of, 45
Constable arrests Joseph Smith, Jr.,
    30–31
Continuing revelation, 148
Copley, Leman, 54–55; withdraws land
    offer, 59
Corrill, John, 93, 104
Cowdery, Elizabeth Ann Whitmer, 23–
    24
Cowdery, Oliver: recounts receiving the
    preface, 2; describes visions of
    Joseph Smith, 6–7; arrives in
    Harmony, 13–14; revelations
    directed to, 14; rejoins the Church,
    14–15; ordained by John the
    Baptist, 19; testimony of, 20–21; as
    a witness, 22–23, 143; ordained by
    Joseph Smith, 26; baptizes converts,